天 文 圖（摹本） 圖二三

SpaceShots

SpaceShots

The Beauty of Nature Beyond Earth

✶ ✶ ✶

TIMOTHY FERRIS

WITH PHOTOGRAPHS SELECTED BY TIMOTHY FERRIS

AND CAROYLN ZECCA

PANTHEON BOOKS

New York

LIBRARY OF CONGRESS CATALOGING IN PUBLICATION DATA

Ferris, Timothy.
Spaceshots: the beauty of nature beyond earth.

Bibliography p.
1. Space photography.   I. Title.
TR713.F47   1984   778.3′5   84–42705
ISBN 0–394–53890–0

Designed by Vincent Winter

MANUFACTURED IN ITALY

First Edition

*The realities of nature
surpass our most ambitious dreams.*

—RODIN

Preface and Acknowledgments

T HIS BOOK PRESENTS scientific photographs in an art format. The paradox is that most of the photographs were taken without an aesthetic intent; indeed, many were taken by automated spacecraft operated by on-board computers at distances of billions of miles from the nearest human being. The captions at the back of the book concern themselves with the scientific content of the photographs, while the introduction investigates the curious question of why they are capable of being beautiful.

During the many hours I've spent since boyhood gazing at photographs of other worlds, I've found that they are customarily employed to illustrate something, usually an explanation of what we know about astronomy or cosmology. They do this well, but every gain involves a loss, and the loss in using the pictures as illustrations is that they become subservient to the text. Lost is a sense of the profound sovereignty of the things in themselves. We on Earth have managed to learn a little about the universe, but it seems to me that our learning ornaments the universe and not the other way round. So in this book I've tried to keep the words out of the way of the pictures.

The photographs were selected by Carolyn Zecca and myself from a quarter of a million images in the archives of the Johnson Space Center in Houston and the Jet Propulsion Laboratory in Pasadena, the libraries of a number of astronomical observatories in the United States, Australia, and West Germany, and from the collections of amateur astronomers and of amateur and professional photographers. Carolyn also supervised much of the sequencing of the photographs, came up with the title of the book, and contributed design suggestions, for which I am in her debt.

I am grateful as well to the photographers, scientists, and engineers whose work created the photographs, and to all those who helped with the book, especially Wendy Goldwyn, my patient and perceptive editor; the indefatigable Mike Gentry of the Johnson Space Center; Ron Weber of Rice University's Lunar and Planetary Institute; my research assistants Pat Brierton and Steve Trainoff; Leslie Pieri, Valerie Nelson, and Jurrie Van Der Woude of the Jet Propulsion Laboratory; Helen Knudson of the Caltech Astrophysics Library; George Preston, John Bedke, and Rhea Goodwin of the Mount Wilson and Las Campanas Observatories; Donald Osterbrock and Robert Kraft of Lick Observatory; Lloyd Carter of the Naval Research Laboratory; Stephen Meszaros and Agnes Paulsen of Kitt Peak National Observatory; Robert Brucato of Palomar Observatory; and to Leif Robinson and Bill Shawcross of *Sky & Telescope* magazine for their aid in contacting amateur astronomers. Thanks go as well to Vincent Winter for his gracious consultation and expert hand in designing the book, and to Diane Best for coloring the ancient Chinese star map reproduced on the endpapers.

T.F.

Los Angeles, California, 1984

Introduction

THE COURTSHIP DANCE

When I have arranged a bouquet for the purpose of painting it,
I always turn to the side I did not plan.
—RENOIR, TO MATISSE

WHY IS NATURE BEAUTIFUL? That question, old when Lucretius wrote lovingly of lowing cattle and scudding clouds, reasserts itself with fresh immediacy now that we have caught a glimpse of nature on the cosmic scale and have found beauty there as well. Lucretius thought that the sun and stars hung low overhead, swimming through the air, very much a part of the earth. We since have learned that the awful truth is otherwise—that the distance to the sun is more than a marathon champion could run in ten thousand years, that the stars are millions of times more distant still, that ours is but one among innumerable worlds careering through space, supremely indifferent to human affairs. And yet the better the look we have at nature on the large scale, the more beauty it reveals. The hellish molten sulphur lakes of Jupiter's satellite Io, photographed at close range by the *Voyager* spacecraft in the images reproduced in Photographs 59 to 61 in this book, display an originality of color and line reminiscent of Miró; the frozen, wind-blasted canyons of Mars (Photograph

57) resemble the faded wash of Etruscan walls; the vaporous remains of a stellar explosion that could have terminated entire planets (Photograph 71) looks comely as a dancer's veil. Why should the sight of remote realms like these arouse our sense of beauty?

Before we try to answer this question, we should ask two others. One is whether we honestly can agree that nature is beautiful. We say as much, but we as a species plunder nature with both hands, and we've been doing so since before the dawn of civilization. The ancient Greeks saw gods in every glen, but that didn't stop them from clearing the land; when Socrates strolled the banks of the Ilissus he was admiring a landscape that had already been stripped to the bone by centuries of man-made soil erosion, leaving what Plato likened to "the skeleton of a sick man, all the fat and soft earth having wasted away." The gently rolling hills of northern Italy had been clear-cut for timber by the time the painters of the Italian Renaissance showed up to immortalize their beauty. The first white men to set eyes on a giant redwood tree immediately cut it down and held a dance that night on its stump. The industrialized societies that today pay homage to the beauty of the wild in their books and television programs are busy destroying virgin Amazon rain forest so rapidly that hundreds of thousands of species of plants and animals are being driven into extinction before they can even be catalogued.

In light of all this, doesn't our praise of natural beauty ring hollow? As William Morris asked a century ago in his book *The Beauty of Life*, "How can you care about the image of a landscape, when you show by your deeds that you don't care for the landscape itself?"

Yet the dark side is not the whole story. It simply suggests that the courtship dance with nature involves backward as well as forward steps, that like many another love affair, it can be freighted with selfishness and a lust for conquest. Little that is human is pure, and no one's love of natural beauty need be called counterfeit just because we live in an imperfect world.

The other preliminary question is what beauty actually is. I don't know the answer. It comforts me that Tolstoy didn't, either. He worked for fifteen years writing a book on art, only to conclude that "the meaning of the word beauty remains an enigma still." Let's say, as Augustine said of time, that we know what beauty is until we are asked to define it.

We can, however, identify one attribute of beauty that is meaningful to art and science alike: that beauty unifies. As Aquinas said, beauty involves unity in diversity. A beautiful painting, or symphony, or differential equation, draws together its parts to form a pleasing whole. A great work of art embraces us, arousing a sense of the interconnectedness of the universe. If the subject is nature, as in Shen Chou's "Walking with a Staff" or Henri

"THE WATERFALL." *Henri Rousseau.*

Rousseau's "The Waterfall," it can show us ourselves as a thread in a seamless natural tapestry.

Science too involves a love of unity. As Jacob Bronowski writes in his book *The Common Sense of Science*, "The constant urge of science as well as the arts is to broaden the likeness for which we grope under the facts. When we discover the wider likeness, whether between space and time, or between the bacillus, the cirrus and the crystal, we enlarge the order in the universe; but more than this, we enlarge its unity."

But why, seeking a sense of unity with nature at large, do we find it? Why does science work, and why do we find beauty amid the wild diversity of the scattered stars?

✦ ✦ ✦

THE AUTHORSHIP OF BEAUTY

In the midst of the world the creator said to Adam, "I have placed thee so thou could look around so much easier, and see all that is in it. . . ."
—Pico della Mirandola

Beauty is truth, truth beauty
—Keats, "Ode on a Grecian Urn"

HISTORY OFFERS two enduring answers to the question of why we find beauty in nature. One, theological in character, identifies beauty with the good and attributes natural beauty to God's authorship of the world. The other identifies the beautiful with the true.

The theological argument holds that God created the universe to suit His own taste ("God saw that it was good"), that He created Man in His image, and that, consequently, the world is pleasing to human as well as to divine perception. Saint Augustine saw the creation of the universe as springing from "the will of a good God that good things should be," and in a passage in Book X of the *Confessions*, itself beautiful, Augustine describes how he was led by his sense of natural beauty to contemplate God's creation of the universe:

I asked the earth, and it answered me, "I am not He"; and whatsover are in it confessed the same. I asked the sea, and the deeps, and the living creeping things, and they answered, "We are not thy God, seek above us." I asked the moving air; and the whole air with his inhabitants answered, "Anaximenes was deceived, I am not God." I asked the heavens, sun, moon, stars, "Nor [say they] are we the God Whom thou seekest." And I replied unto all the things which encompass the door of my flesh; "Ye have told me of my God, that ye are not He; tell me something of Him." And they cried out with a loud voice, "He made us." My questioning them was my thoughts on them: and their form of beauty gave the answer.

Augustine's reverent outlook might seem to have lost currency in a scientific age, but the genesis of modern science owes a lot to his brand of religious faith. In their efforts to find simple, logical principles in the workings of nature, the architects of modern science were sustained by a faith that God had built the world rationally, just as He had bedecked it in beauty. Johannes Kepler, the discoverer of the laws of planetary motion, discarded seventy erroneous hypotheses in the course of years of research before he realized that the orbits of the planets are ellipses; but he seems never to have doubted that an answer could be found, and that when it was found it would be elegantly simple and beautiful. He believed, as Einstein would put it three hundred years later, that God is subtle but not malicious. When Kepler's faith had been rewarded, he wrote of the system of orbital dynamics that had been revealed to him, "I contemplate its beauty with incredible and ravishing delight," and he concluded his book *De Harmonice Mundi* with a grateful prayer:

> O Thou Who dost by the light of nature promote in us the desire for the light of grace, that by its means Thou mayest transport us into the light of glory, I give thanks to Thee, O Lord Creator, Who hast delighted me with Thy makings and in the works of Thy hands have I exulted. . . .

Resilient as faith itself, the theological argument can be employed in reverse, to reason that the beauty of the world proves the existence of an omniscient and splendid God, creator of the universe. "The heavens declare the glory of God, and the firmament sheweth His handiwork," as Psalm 19 puts it. Nature's wonders demonstrate God's boundless glory and love for the world—"the love," in Dante's phrase, "which moves the sun and the other stars."

This was Isaac Newton's view. "This most beautiful system of the sun, planets, and comets," he wrote in the *Principia,*

> could only proceed from the counsel and dominion of an intelligent and powerful Being. . . . And from his true dominion it follows that the true God is a living, intelligent, and powerful Being. . . . eternal and infinite, omnipotent and omniscient; that is, his duration reaches from eternity to eternity; his presence from infinity to infinity; he governs all things, and knows all things that are or can be done.

Yet despite its grandeur and its illustrious history, the theological argument ultimately fails to prove the existence of God, and, therefore, since it attributes natural beauty to God and to no other cause, it cannot in itself explain why nature is beautiful. It is a subspecies of what Immanuel Kant in his *Critique of Pure Reason* called the "physico-theological proof," and it was Kant who dug its grave. He approached it with deference. "This argument," he wrote, "always deserves to be mentioned with respect. It is the oldest, the clearest, and the most in conformity with the common reason of humanity. It animates the study of nature, as it itself derives its existence and draws ever new strength from that source." Nevertheless, he found, it is "insufficient of itself to prove the existence of a Supreme Being. . . ."

Its limitation, Kant saw, is that our appreciation of God the artist is of necessity rooted in a human concept of art, a concept too meager to suffice as proof of the existence of an all-powerful God. We finite, mortal beings lack what Kant called a "proportionate" idea grand enough to establish the existence of Newton's "eternal and infinite, omnipotent and omniscient" God. As Kant writes,

> It cannot be expected that anyone will be bold enough to declare that he has a perfect insight into the relation which the magnitude of the world he contemplates bears (in its extent as well as in its content) to omnipotence, into that of the order and design in the world to the highest wisdom, and that of the unity of the world to the absolute unity of a Supreme Being. . . . Thus this argument is utterly insufficient for the task before us—a demonstration of the existence of an all-sufficient being.

If the existence of beauty fails to prove the existence of God, then we cannot explain beauty solely by attributing it to God.

The second argument, that nature is beautiful because nature is true, has

"THE STARRY NIGHT." *Vincent Van Gogh.*

been around for a long time; the conviction that beauty involves correspondence to the truth is one of the few constant threads in the tangled history of aesthetics. But what kind of truth engenders beauty? It cannot be the merely literal truth that Freud defined as "correspondence with the real external world." It is the beauty of the natural world that we are trying to explain; to define it as correspondence to reality is to reason in a circle. And, if we really thought that an accurate portrayal of the surface appearances of nature was beautiful by definition, then every clearly focused snapshot would be beautiful. But astronomers make accurate photographs of the stars every night, and few, if any, of them are as beautiful as, say, Van Gogh's painting "Starry Night." Nor is the Van Gogh canvas "true," if by truth we mean strict correspondence with the outer appearances of the external world.

It resembles no photograph of the night sky, nor was Van Gogh particularly interested in that sort of truth.*

Even those artists who define art as but an imitation of nature agree that what they are imitating is something deeper than the surface appearances of nature. Paul Klee felt that the artist tries to "dig down close to the secret source where the primal law feeds the forces of development," and there, at the roots of reality, we find not literal truth but something deeper and considerably harder to define. It is the truth that Lao Tzu called the Way, and which, he said, could not be put in words: "The Way that can be told is not the eternal Way," reads the first sentence of the *Tao Te Ching*. It is the truth that Jesus of Nazareth, asked by Pilate, "What is truth?" defined with silence.

Perhaps, then, the mystery of mystical truth is also the mystery of beauty. It is frightening in that it is unknown and perhaps unknowable and cannot be captured in words, numbers, or concepts—though these may open a window through which we perceive at least part of the truth, and through which, therefore, shines beauty. As Rilke wrote, "Beauty's nothing but the start of terror we can hardly bear. . . ." Nikos Kazantzakis wrote that beauty "is merciless. You do not look at it, it looks at you and does not forgive."

But, like the theological argument, the statement that beauty is truth rests upon a mystical conception that is immune to logical analysis or precise definition. This does not mean that the argument is false, only that it has its limits. If we seek an explanation that casts its net as widely as does nature itself, we must look further.

* As it happens we know what Van Gogh had in mind in this instance, as he wrote about the painting to his brother Theo: "This picture raises the eternal question whether we can see the whole of life or only know a hemisphere of it before death. I've no idea of the answer myself. But the sight of stars always sets me dreaming just as naïvely as those black dots on a map set me dreaming of towns and villages. Why should those points of light in the firmament, I wonder, be less accessible than the dark ones on the map of France? We take a train to go to Tarascon or Rouen and we take death to go to a star."

↑   ↑   ↑

THE EVOLUTION OF BEAUTY

*The light which we have gained was given us, not to be ever
starting on, but by it to discover onward things more remote from
our knowledge.*

—MILTON, *Areopagitica*

A THIRD HYPOTHESIS holds that we were selected, in the course of our evolution, for an aesthetic sense, much as we were selected for intelligence or physical fitness or our attractiveness to the opposite sex.

We know that random genetic variations produce, within any given population of any species, some individuals who are more likely than others to survive long enough to reproduce, passing their genetic advantage along to their young. That, in essence, is how evolution works. Natural selection explains gross features of anatomy and physiology, such as why polar bears have white coats (camouflaged, they do better at stalking seals in the snow), and why bucks have antlers (the better his weapons, the better the buck is able to keep other males from his harem). Evolution theory has not, of course, explained every subtle characteristic of every species, but this does not mean that there is anything fundamentally wrong with the theory; life is so rich and diverse, and our knowledge of its evolutionary history so scanty, that we have as yet hardly scratched the surface. Many if not all physical and psychological characteristics of animals presumably can be understood in terms of evolution, once we know enough about them.

The human ability to see beauty in nature could very well be one such characteristic. Briefly put, the argument is that the likelihood of our ancestors surviving to puberty and having children was influenced to some degree by the extent to which they actually *liked* it here on Earth.

Darwin's discussions of the sense of beauty concentrated upon its role in mating: Men are more inclined to mate with women they find beautiful, and vice versa; and this process, repeated down through the generations, accounts for the strong sense of beauty that can be aroused in each of us by the sight of a particularly comely individual of the opposite sex. (Tastes vary, of course, but it's the inclination that matters here, not the particulars of its satisfaction.) The evolution of a nature aesthetic, however, would have involved a wider range of interactions between our ancestors and the natural world than the data of human history yet permit us to reconstruct. The processes involved are sufficiently complex and subtle that we can at present do little more than speculate about them. But it does seem reasonable to suppose that, generally speaking, people are rather more likely to get along well in life if they take some pleasure in their surroundings. The best mushroom-gatherer is the one who loves mushrooms, and the best hunter is the one who likes hunting; and one way to excel at the hunt is to crave the pleasure of seeing the prey. Anthropologists speculate that twenty-thousand-year-old cave paintings, like those in Lascaux near Montignac, the sight of which inspired Picasso, were drawn as part of a magic ritual intended to promote success in the hunt; but what is not speculative about them is that they are beautiful.

If the individual who sees only ugliness in nature will, especially if living in a state of nature, be vulnerable to a variety of disasters—among them simple mishap, psychosomatic disease, or parental or social neglect encouraged by his own disagreeableness—he who sees beauty in the world resonates with nature, in a kind of Keplerian harmony, and is nourished by the world. An aesthetically sensitive child might, then as now, be subject to rejection—William Blake as a boy was punished by his father for reporting that he had seen angels perched in a tree—but generally speaking, a conviction that there is beauty in nature would seem to enhance one's chances for a happy and (re)productive life.

The evolution of a sense of natural beauty could have promoted not just art but science as well. The creative scientist studies nature with the rapt gaze of the lover, and is guided as often by aesthetic as by rational considerations in guessing at how nature works. "A scientist worthy of the name, above all a mathematician, experiences in his work the same impression as an artist," said Henri Poincaré, the mathematician and theoretical astronomer. "His pleasure is as great and of the same nature." Paul Dirac, one of the inventors of quantum physics, said that "it is more important to have beauty in one's equations than to have them fit experiment. . . . You feel it, just like beauty in a picture or beauty in music." Richard Feynman, creator of the Feynman diagrams ubiquitously employed in theoretical particle physics, goes so far as to say that "to those who do not know mathematics it is difficult to get across a real feelings as to the beauty, the deepest beauty, of nature."

Unlike the two explanations of natural beauty we encountered earlier—one attributing the beauty of nature to God's artistry, the other to an equation linking beauty and truth—the evolutionary hypothesis does not envision a fundamental disjunction dividing nature from the human mind. The theological argument sees Man as set down in a precreated Eden with which he is linked solely by his and the garden's common origin at the hand of God. The argument of beauty as truth sees communication between Man and the outside world as possible, owing to an inexplicable, perhaps miraculous communion of mind (or soul) with a disinterested natural world. But the evolutionary hypothesis says that we are at one with the world, kin to every living thing on earth, and it sees our sense of natural beauty as a kind of resonance between ourselves, our fellow creatures, and the planet that gave birth to us all. In this its unifying tendency it echoes the sentiment voiced by artists who say they feel that in making art they are part of nature. Paul Klee portrayed the artist as a tree, his roots sunk into nature, the crown his art—"The beauty at the crown is not his own," he wrote. "He is merely a channel"—and Hans Arp told Mondrian, "Art is of natural origin."* Darwin's discovery of evolution by natural selection invites us to consider that the artist's sense of kinship with the wider world can find support not only in opinion but by empirically verifiable fact, that the course of our evolution may have produced inclinations as subtle as those we lump together under the rubric of aesthetics.

The limitation of the evolutionary hypothesis, other than its purely speculative quality, is that while it may ultimately help account for our aesthetic appreciation of this one planet, it cannot in itself explain the appeal of realms beyond the earth. Why, if we evolved on this world alone and have known no other, do we sense a kinship between the mountains of Earth and the mountains of Mars, and find beauty in the stars?

* Hegel disagreed with the thrust of this argument. He wondered why, if nature is beautiful and art aspires to closer contact with its beauties, the artist should bother to create something that nature already supplies. But this is rather like asking why we bother dancing at a dance.

✓ ✓ ✓

ODYSSEUS' POLAROID

The heroic mind . . . has no doubt that what it sees is real.
—JOHN H. FINLEY, JR.,
Four Stages of Greek Thought

FOR MOST OF HUMAN HISTORY, our view of the universe was limited to what could be seen in the sky with the unaided eye—the sun and moon, five planets and some ten thousand stars in our galaxy, and the indistinct glow of three galaxies beyond the Milky Way. These sights are splendid enough to have inspired many a poet (Shakespeare invoked the moon and stars over two hundred times, and he wasn't especially interested in the night sky), but they amount to less than one one-hundred-billionth of the universe. Restricted to a paucity of data, early astronomers assumed that the sky was a low roof and the stars but its ornaments.

All that changed on the summer evening in 1609 when Galileo trained a telescope on the skies. The moon, he saw, looked not like a wafer but like a *planet*, with rugged mountains and broad plains resembling those of Earth. Jupiter had moons of its own, and the Milky Way resolved itself into an "almost unbelievable" profusion of stars. Here was evidence that the extra-terrestrial universe was not a decorated dome but a theater of worlds, of real places, ultimately as susceptible to exploration and investigation as the islands of the West Indies. Within four centuries after Kepler wrote Galileo to suggest in his whimsical way that they could fly to the planets, men had set foot on the moon.

Early telescopic astronomers like Galileo, Newton, and William Herschel frequently remarked on the great beauty of the universe, though what they could see of it was still quite limited. Except for the planets, the brighter stars of the Milky Way, and a few of the most conspicuous nebulae and galaxies, everything in the sky is too dim to be perceived in any detail by the eye, even through a powerful telescope. A full appreciation of cosmic beauty came only with the wedding of the camera to the telescope. Time-exposure photographs made through large telescopes recorded much more light than the eye ever could. For the first time, human beings could behold in full detail the spiderweb filaments of wrecked stars, the glowing nebulous reefs and shoals of the Milky Way, and the thickets of galaxies stretching away endlessly into deep space.

The origins of astrophotography date from those of photography itself. It was an astronomer, John Herschel, who coined the word "photography," and who invented the fixing process used in the darkroom ever since. The first man to take a daguerreotype portrait of a human face—John William Draper, who in 1839 persuaded his devoted wife, Dorothy, to sit still for a half-hour exposure, her face dusted with white powder to make it reflect light—was also the first to take a photograph of the moon, the following year. Early plates were too insensitive to be of much use in recording images of anything but the moon, the sun, and the brightest stars; but they improved, and on September 30, 1880, Draper's son Henry, using one of the new dry plates fitted to a twelve-inch refracting telescope at his observatory at Hastings-on-Hudson, New York, obtained the first successful photograph of the Orion Nebula, a glowing cloud of gas sixteen hundred light years from Earth. (For a modern representation of the Orion Nebula, see Photograph 63.) The Orion Nebula had long tantalized visual observers, for whom it took on various forms, depending upon how much of its faint outer reaches they could make out through a given telescope on a given night. Ainslie Common in England helped resolve the question when in 1882 he photographed dim outer filaments of the nebula invisible to the human eye, demonstrating that it was far more extensive than had been thought. A long-exposure, wide-field photograph by E. E. Bernard in California then showed the nebula as but a knot in an even larger tangle of nebulosity embracing the entire constellation of Orion. The long, sinuous structure unveiled in these early astrophotographs was nothing less than one of the spiral arms that stretch for thousands of light years along the disk of our galaxy.

Astronomical photographs soon became as popular for their aesthetics as for their intellectual appeal. Widely reproduced in books and magazines, the sights of deep space in general and of spiral galaxies in particular came to be regarded, like the Alps, as symbols of the awestruck, aesthetic epiphany that Kant had called "the Sublime," and had defined as involving "a representation of limitlessness." If a single galaxy, like the Andromeda Galaxy, the sweeping spiral arms of which were revealed by Isaac Roberts in an 1888 photograph, was sublime, how much more so was the vista captured by J. E. Keeler in 1895, at the Lick Observatory in California, when he photographed thousands of spiral "nebulae," each a galaxy in its own right, strewn across the depths of space. The aesthetic and technical merit of astronomical photographs improved together, and it became something of a maxim in astronomy that the more clearly one could see an object in space, the more beautiful it looked.

Among the most talented astrophotographers was the optician George Ritchey, a perfectionist who often spent three full nights guiding the sixty-inch Mount Wilson telescope in order to expose a single plate. When more sensitive but grainier photographic emulsions became available, Ritchey stuck to the older, slower emulsions, preferring their high contrast and high resolution. His portraits of the galaxy M33, the Veil Nebula, and the globular star cluster in Hercules—sharp and clear, their bone-white stars set against a bottomless black sky—brought millions into contact with the grandeur and beauty of nature on the large scale.

GALAXY NGC-598 (M-33).
AUGUST 5–7, 1910.
George Ritchey.

Color came to astrophotography in the 1950s. Its pioneer was William Miller of the Mount Wilson and Palomar observatories. The chief technical obstacle Miller had to overcome was that the three layers of emulsion employed in color film, one for each of the primary colors, differ markedly in their sensitivity to light in the course of the long exposures required to photograph galaxies and nebulae. The color imbalances resulting from this problem, called reciprocity failure, could not be corrected by comparing trial photographs with the objects themselves, since nearly all deep-space objects are too dim to activate the color receptors of the eye. As Miller wrote, "We do not know what nebulae and galaxies should look like in color, for we have never seen and probably never shall see them visually in their true colors." Miller conducted laboratory tests to graph the inaccuracies of the color film, corrected for them by using filters, and produced what still rank among the most accurate deep-space color astrophotographs ever made. (For Miller's portrait of the Andromeda Galaxy, see Photograph 74.)

Soon cameras were being lofted into space. This brought them no closer to the stars—going all the way to Pluto reduces one's distance to the very nearest star by only two one-hundredths of one percent—but it made possible remarkably detailed photography of the moon and planets. The far side of the moon, never before seen by man, began yielding up its ancient secrets in 1959, when the Soviet *Luna* 3 probe swung round the moon. Soft landings by the automated *Luna* 9 and *Surveyor* 1 probes in 1966 produced close-up, black-and-white photographs of the lunar surface. Snapshots taken on the moon by the Apollo astronauts, in the series of missions beginning when Neil Armstrong set foot on virgin lunar soil on July 20, 1969, demonstrated that the lunar landscape, for all its airless severity, has a ghostly beauty all its own.

Close-up views of the planets produced an aesthetic impact that had been foreseen by only a few scientists and science-fiction writers and by visionaries like Chesley Bonestell, the painter of extraterrestrial landscapes. Mars, photographed most spectacularly by the Viking orbiters and landers dispatched there in 1975, was revealed as a world of delicate hues, its ocher sand dunes leavened by paper-white snowdrifts, its mist-filled canyons washed with the colors of a rusting freighter. (See Photographs 56 and 58.) Jupiter displayed a carnival abundance of red, white, and blue cloud bands suggestive of a hot-air balloon. The twin *Voyager* spacecraft that imaged Jupiter continued on to Saturn, a chillier and more austere world, whose chief extravagance proved to be the broad golden causeway of its celebrated ring system (Photographs 10, 11, 4, 5).

During its encounter with Jupiter, *Voyager* transmitted back images of the Jovian satellites Europa and Callisto, with their mighty oceans sheathed in ice, Ganymede (Photographs 8, 9) splotched with ammonia white and the tarnished browns of a Roman coin, and the seething volcanoes and sulphur lakes of Io (Photographs 59 to 61). At Saturn, where the sun, a billion miles distant, glows with the faded warmth of candlelight, *Voyager* recorded the gentle beiges and pearl tones of cratered moons like Tethys, Rhea, Enceladus, and Dione, the carbon-blotched face of Iapetus, and the caramel-colored fog that hides the face of the giant moon Titan (Photograph 6).

Astrophotography promoted a renewal of what might be called the aesthetic of the explorer—what John Finley describes, with reference to Homer, as "an outgazing bent of mind that sees things exactly, each for itself, and seems innocent of the idea that thought discerps and colors reality." As Finley writes:

> When in the sixth book of the *Iliad* Hector briefly returns to Troy from the battlefield and in a famous scene meets his wife and infant son at the gate and reaches out to take the boy in his arms, the child draws back frightened at his father's bronze armor and helmet with horsehair crest; whereupon Hector laughs, takes off the helmet, and lays it all-shining on the

ground. In so deeply felt a scene surely no one but Homer would have paused to note that helmet still shining beside the human figures. It is as if in whatever circumstances, it too keeps its particular being, which does not change because people are sad or happy but remains what it is, one of the innumerable fixed entities that comprise the world.

The new views of the planets, stars, and galaxies helped awaken the world to the existential sovereignty of these other worlds; they directed our attention outward. And that attention, like Kepler's, was rewarded when the wider universe turned out to be not only scientifically interesting but compellingly beautiful as well.

But the attention paid to the beauty of the universe only deepened the mystery of the nature aesthetic. For Homer there was no such mystery; the objects he described were indisputably of this world: Hector's helmet was Hector's, the sea and the stars part of humanity's home. But we are confronted by gulfs of space deeper than any Homer described and by worlds stranger than the cave of the Cyclops, and no theory of a Darwinian evolution of aesthetics can explain why our eye should delight at these strange sights. Our ancestors, never having seen, say, the Tarantula Nebula in the Large Magellanic Cloud (Photograph 73), could hardly have been selected for any preference in this regard, and evolution proceeds much too slowly to have had any effect in the scant century or so that has elapsed since astrophotography began to acquaint us with the splendors of nature at large. If we are to account for the phenomenon of the beauty of the universe we need look for answers where the question arises, out among the stars themselves.

✤   ✤   ✤

RULES OF THE GAME

The dance along the artery
The circulation of the lymph
Are figured in the drift of stars.
                    —T. S. ELIOT

EINSTEIN USED TO SAY that the most inexplicable thing about the universe is that it is explicable. Why should the human brain be able to probe the nucleus of the carbon atom or chart the wanderings of the Whirlpool Galaxy (Photograph 66)? Historically, attempts to answer this question have involved lines of reasoning that parallel those invoked to explain why nature is beautiful. Newton attributed the intelligibility of nature to the grace of God; the Taoists in China saw natural order as part of a deep, unutterable truth uniting mind and nature; and, more recently, an evolutionary hypothesis was invoked, when it was suggested that a life spent swinging from branch to branch, with the severe penalties such a practice imposes upon failure, helped inculcate in our primate ancestors an intuitive sense of the nature of gravity. The evolutionary hypothesis does not explain why life or intelligence arose in the first place, but it does offer clues as to how the human mind might have evolved in such harmony with its surroundings that we are able both to sense the beauty of nature, and, through science, to understand something of how nature functions.

Having found both beauty and intelligibility in nature here on earth, we could extend our appreciation and understanding into realms beyond the earth, if in fact nature everywhere works according to the same rules. And that it does so is just what science has found. The spectroscope reveals that nitrogen atoms in the atmosphere of Mars are identical to nitrogen atoms in the atmosphere of the earth; that hydrogen gas in quasars, billions of light years away, behaves just like hydrogen in the laboratory; that the gravity that tugs the apple from the tree also binds the galaxies together. The allegedly universal laws of physics, science finds, really are universal, and hold sway throughout the cosmos. The universality of natural laws builds a bridge that links our little world to the rest of the cosmos.

But how can natural law function universally? As the astrophysicist and philosopher Arthur Stanley Eddington used to put it, how does an electron "know" that it's an electron, that it should behave exactly like electrons on the other side of the universe?

Until recently, science had no answer to this question. Then, in 1929, came the discovery of the expansion of the universe. At Mount Wilson Observatory, Edwin Hubble, with the aid of his colleague Milton Humason, and employing additional data garnered by Vesto Slipher of the Lowell Observatory in Arizona, discovered that the light from distant galaxies is shifted toward the red end of the spectrum by a degree directly proportional to the distance of each galaxy. The only wholly consistent explanation for this phenomenon is that the universe is expanding—that the red shift of light from galaxies is caused by the galaxies' hurtling apart from one another. Such velocities stretch out the light waves, making them appear to be lower in frequency—redder—just as a car horn sounds lower in pitch if the car is speeding away. In a uniformly expanding universe, an observer in any given galaxy will find that all the other galaxies are receding, and that the further away they are, the faster they are moving. (Imagine that a chessboard, set to begin a game, is expanded to double its original dimensions; the pieces that were furthest apart to begin with—the four rooks—will have to move the fastest to keep up with the expanding board, while those close together, like the black king and black queen, need move only gradually to double the small intervals separating them.) This was just what Hubble saw in the sky. Though he didn't know it at the time, his discovery confirmed a prediction made thirteen years earlier by Einstein's general theory of relativity, which implied that the universe might be expanding.

The evidence for the expansion of the universe is about as imposing as any adduced for a theory of its scope. The rate of expansion of the universe indicates that it began roughly eighteen to twenty billion years ago; this jibes with what astrophysicists estimate to be the ages of the oldest stars in our galaxy, some fifteen to sixteen billion years, and with the five-billion-year age of the solar system induced from the radioactive dating of ancient earth and moon rocks. The "cosmic background radiation"—residual energy left over from the early, energetic phase of expansion of the universe—was detected in 1965, by two American radio astronomers, Arno Pezias and Robert Wilson, and its characteristics fit exactly with those predicted by the theory. Physicists studying the chemistry of the early universe reckoned that about one quarter of the original hydrogen in the universe ought to have been converted into helium; observations of stars establish that, sure enough, they are made of about twenty-five percent helium. Supported by one of the best-established theories in science and confirmed unanimously by subsequent observations, the expansion-of-the- universe theory has ripened into something approaching the status of fact.

Although the theory seemed strange at first—Eddington called it "un-aesthetic"—it promises to clear up his own question of how universal laws got to be universal. If the galaxies are moving apart, they must once, long ago, have all been together. The very early universe must therefore have been a high-density universe, its mass of ten thousand billion billion stars melded together in a state hotter than the center of a star. Few if any of the structures we find in matter today could have maintained themselves under such conditions—not molecules, nor the nuclei of atoms, nor the nucleons that comprise the nucleus—and most of those particles that did exist would have been decaying, interacting, and otherwise carrying on at such a rate that the universe would be a seethe of virtually pure energy. In the primordial ball of fire, the "big bang," the cosmos is said to have blossomed.

There lies redemption for the philosophy of science as well. When Newton asked himself how the stars, strewn far across the reaches of space, could all obey the same laws, he assumed that they always had been strewn across space. In that case, only a transcendent principle like an act of God could account for the universal intelligibility of nature. But the big-bang theory reveals that the stars—and the planets, and everything else—were once all crushed together, in the boiling primordial broth that characterized the universe during the first moments of its expansion. It was just then, when everything in the universe was cheek-by-jowl with everything else, that the particles received their marching orders. We don't fully understand the dynamics of the big bang, and many questions remain to be answered as to how there could have been time for the constituent elements of the cosmos to confer before departing on their divergent trajectories toward the present, but the discovery of the big bang holds out great hope of settling the mystery of the origins of specific universal physical laws. The answer to Eddington's question of why all electrons are alike is that they all got together, back in the big bang, and worked it out among themselves.

✦   ✦   ✦

THE EVOLUTION OF THE UNIVERSE

All things are connected like the blood which unites one family.
—CHIEF SEATTLE

All is like an ocean, all is flowing and blending. . . . It's all like an ocean, I tell you.
—FATHER ZOSSIMA, in *The Brothers Karamazov*

THE FURTHER WE LOOK BACK in time, the simpler nature appears to have been. The early universe must have been relatively homogeneous: Dip a ladle into it when it was, say, one one-hundredth of a second old, and you would find the universe everywhere made of the same boiling soup—mostly photons, electrons and positrons, neutrinos and antineutrinos. Dip a ladle into the universe today, and depending upon where you collected your sample you might come up with a clod of cyanide molecules from the Orion Nebula, a snowball shed by a comet, a toucan's eye, or an ivory key from an organ once played by J. S. Bach. Subatomic particles today can behave much like individual objects—that's why physicists call them particles—but in the crush of the early universe they would instead have behaved like waves of energy, as if the universe were one great tolling bell.

The laws of nature themselves may have evolved from simpler laws, perhaps even from a single, genesic principle that ruled the universe at the beginning of time. Four fundamental forces operate in nature today: the two nuclear forces, called the "strong" and "weak" forces; gravitation, the mutual attraction of matter for matter; and electromagnetism, responsible for light and radio waves and for the fact that atoms can collaborate to form molecules. ("Solid" objects, like the universe at large, are mostly space; it is the electromagnetic bonding holding atoms together that lends objects the illusion of solidity.) Physicists studying these fundamental forces have found that the forces could very well have evolved from a smaller number of forces that functioned in the violent heat of the big bang. When the universe was but 10^{-10} second old, the tasks that today are performed by the electromagnetic and weak forces would have been handled by a single, "electroweak" force. Still earlier, at only 10^{-35} second after the beginning of the big bang, a single, "electronuclear" force could have accounted for all interactions save those involving gravity. Intense study is being devoted to the issue of whether the electronuclear force was once joined with gravitation as well, to form a single, "superunified" interaction.

In short, science has found ample evidence to support the hypothesis that the universe really is a cosmos, a unified whole. Neither life nor thought need be excluded from the circle of cosmic unity. Almost everything that science has been able to learn about the evolution of life and of the universe indicates that both are part of the same immense story, that the universe has erected no walls to segregate the evolution of life and mind from that of nature on the largest scale. The chemical evolution of the cosmos, the formation of the solar system, and the rise of life on Earth form a continuum to which we ourselves evidently belong.

Science, then, draws us into that unity with nature the sensation of which has long been regarded as a quality of art, and shows us why the universe might appear to be both intelligible and beautiful. As a matter of cold empirical fact, as independent from our mystical yearnings as we know how to get, the universe presents itself as all of a piece and tells us that we are part of it. The big bang was about as unified an event as one could imagine, and we were *there*. Every electron in the synapses of every human (and inhuman) thought, every atom of our blood and bones, every *here* was *there*. That was a long time ago, but the unity of the universe remains with us, if only as a species of remembrance, sensed through art and articulated through science. Physics teaches that the unity of nature perceived in art and in our sensations of beauty in nature is a physical unity, traceable back to the origin of the universe, its story unfolding still.

Insofar as the universe is harmonious, our thoughts and perceptions resonate with its harmonies; and insofar as the universe is struggling to complete itself, so are we. This, I think, is akin to what Kant meant when he wrote that when "we call the object beautiful, we believe ourselves to be speaking with a universal voice." It is the source of the "preestablished harmony" to which Leibniz attributed our sense of the beautiful. It is what Alyosha in *The Brothers Karamazov* felt when, staggering out into the night from Father Zossima's deathbed and "weeping even over those stars," he perceived that "there seemed to be threads from all those innumerable worlds of God, linking his soul to them, and it was trembling all over in contact with other worlds." To realize this is not, of course, to have solved the mystery of why the universe exists, or why it has produced offspring capable of thinking about the universe and wondering at its beauty. It is to say that the mystery of our existence, and of that of the cosmos, and of our intellectual and emotional sympathies with the cosmos, are one.

Above:
RODEN CRATER, ARIZONA.
Below:
OLYMPUS MONS, MARS.
James Turrell and Dick Wiser,
NASA JPL.

31

1. EARTH FROM THE SPACE SHUTTLE. *Columbia, NASA.*

2. MARS. *Viking 2, NASA.*

3. ENCELADUS, SATELLITE OF SATURN. *Voyager, NASA.*

4. SATURN AND ITS SATELLITES TETHYS AND DIONE. *Voyager 1, NASA.*

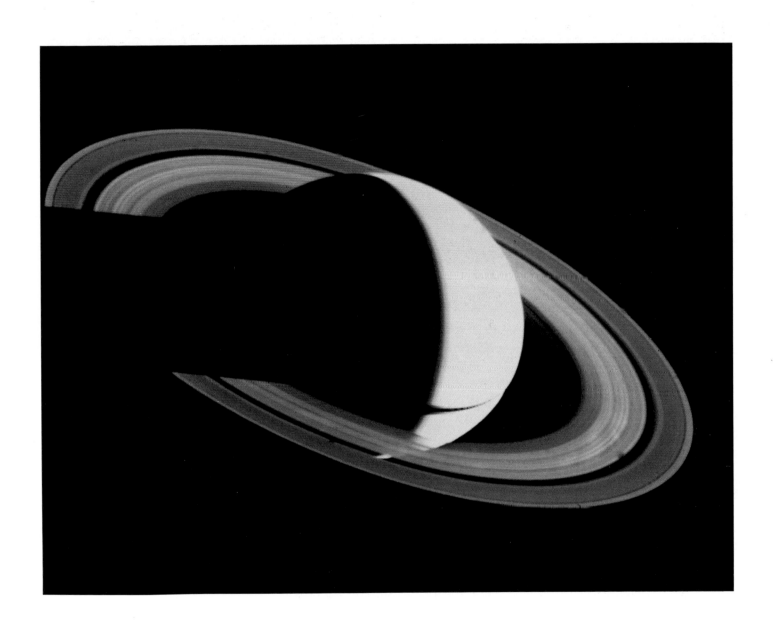

5. FAR SIDE OF SATURN. *Voyager 1*, NASA.

6. HORIZON OF TITAN, SATELLITE OF SATURN. *Voyager, NASA.*

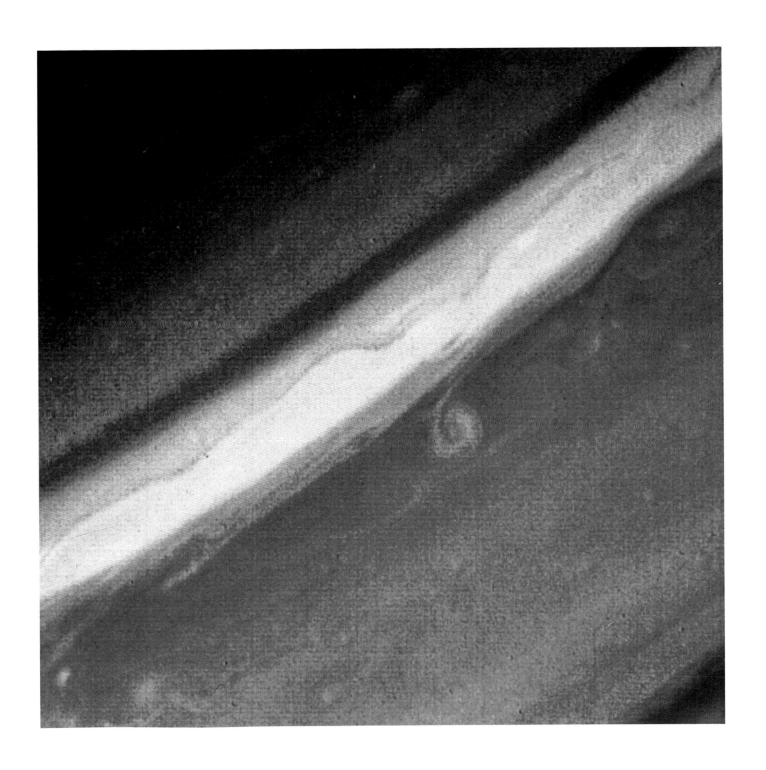

7. SURFACE OF SATURN. *Voyager 2*, NASA.

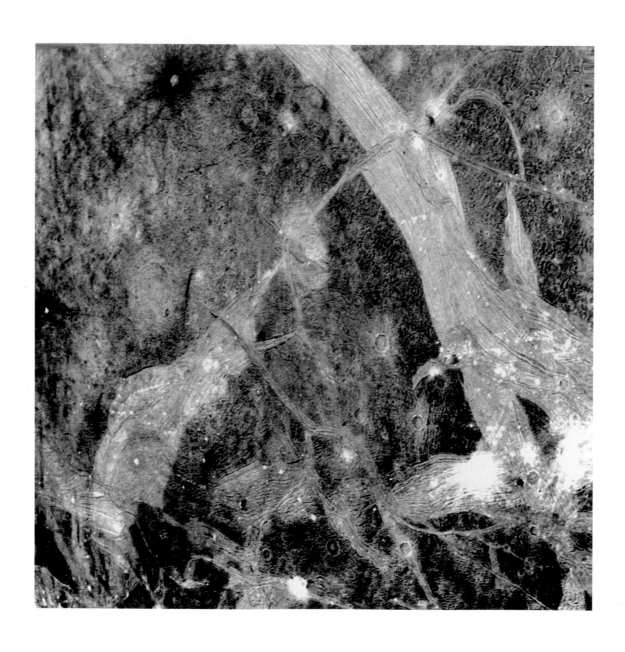

8. GANYMEDE, SATELLITE OF JUPITER. *Voyager, NASA.*

9. GANYMEDE. *Voyager, NASA.*

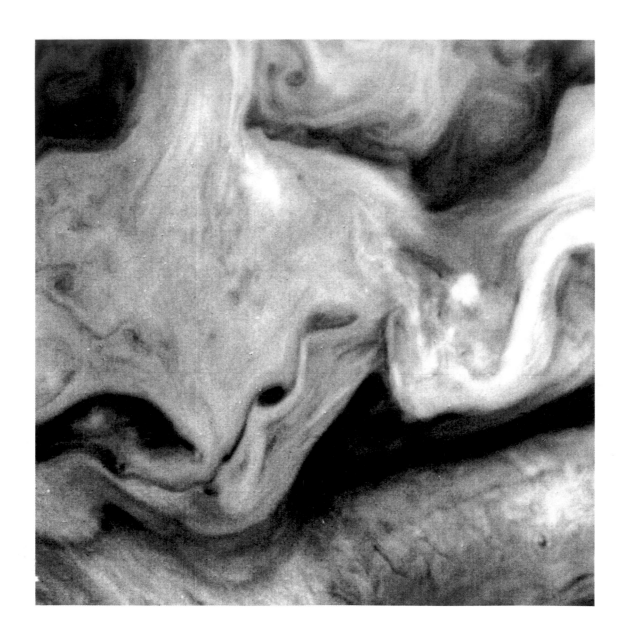

10. SURFACE OF JUPITER. *Voyager, NASA.*

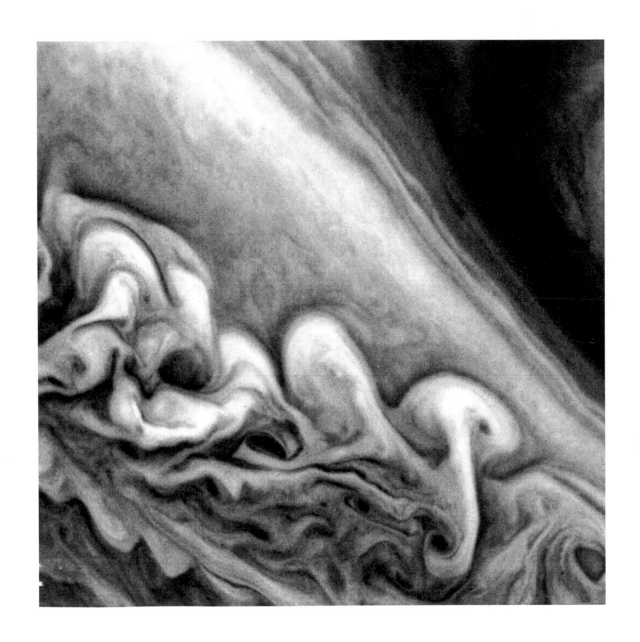

11. **SURFACE OF JUPITER.** *Voyager, NASA.*

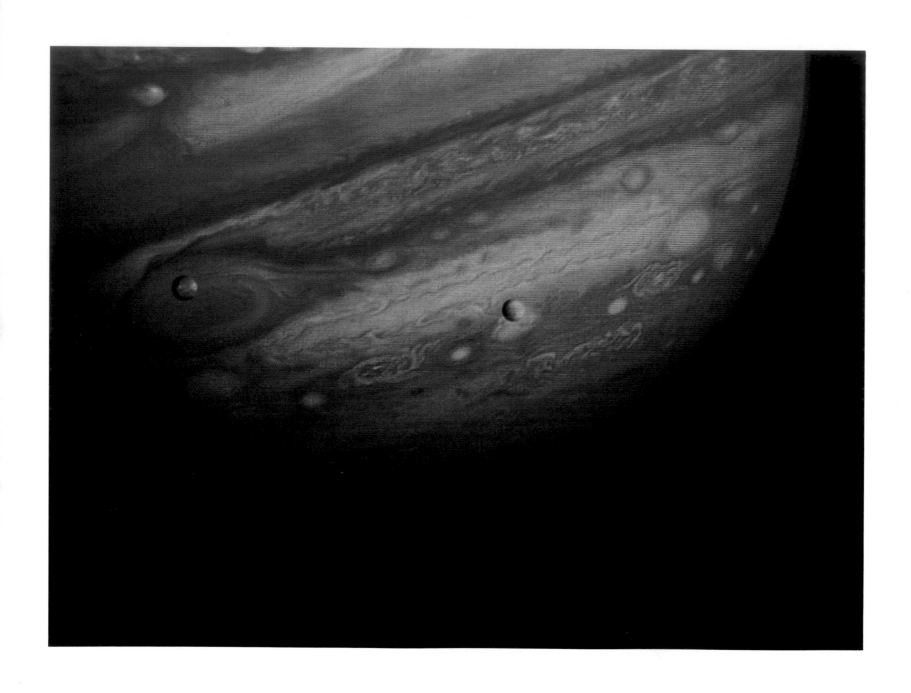

12. JUPITER AND ITS SATELLITES IO AND EUROPA. *Voyager 1, NASA.*

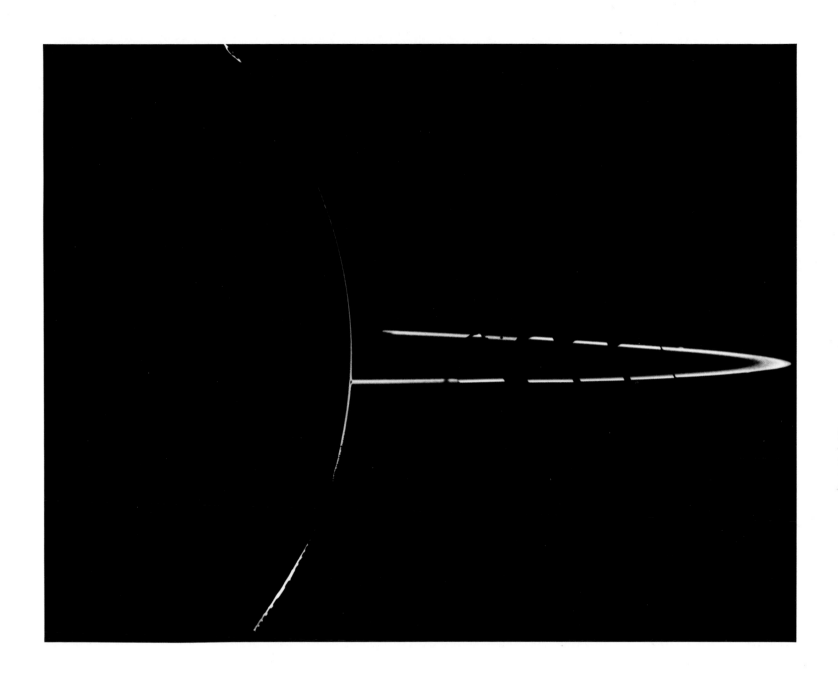

13. JUPITER'S RING. *Voyager 1, NASA.*

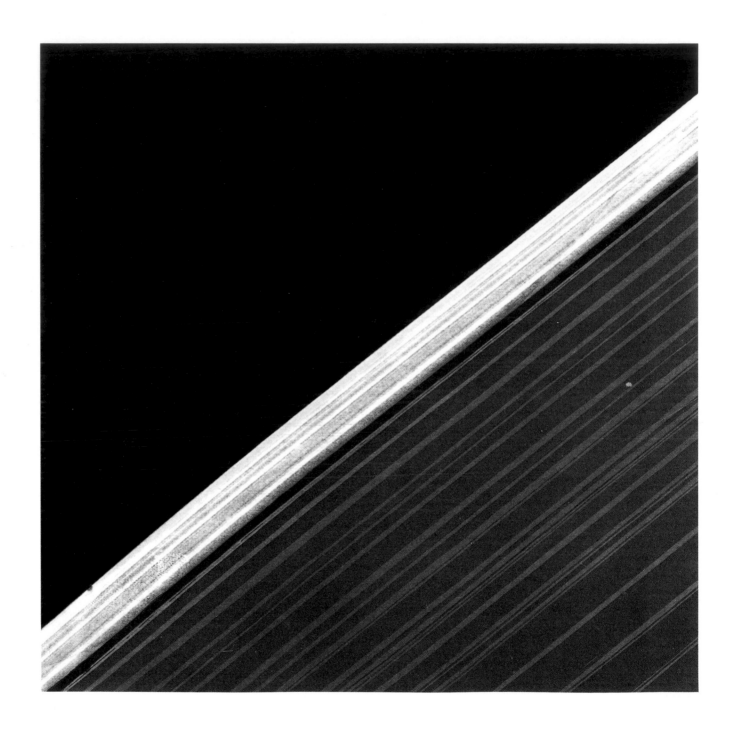

14. SATURN'S RINGS. *Voyager, NASA.*

15. SATURN'S RINGS, FALSE COLOR. *Voyager 1, NASA.*

16. SATURN'S RINGS, FALSE COLOR. *Voyager 2, NASA.*

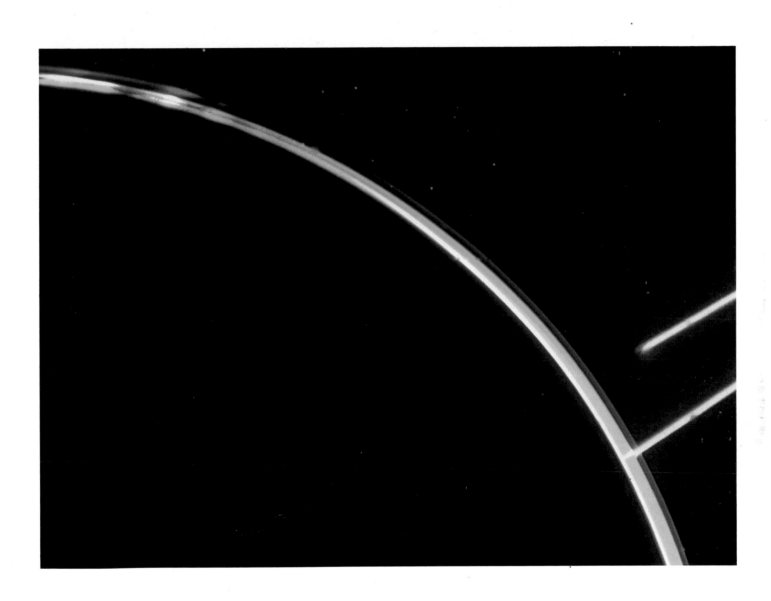

17. JUPITER'S RING. *Voyager 2*, NASA.

18. APOLLO 9 SPACEWALK. *David Scott, NASA.*

19. SECOND MAN ON THE MOON. *Neil Armstrong, NASA.*

20. SKYLAB ASTRONAUT. NASA.

21. UNTETHERED SPACEWALK. *Vance Brand*, NASA.

22. APOLLO IN EARTH ORBIT. *Russell Schweickart, NASA.*

23. APOLLO COMMAND MODULE OVER MOON. *Apollo 10, NASA.*

24. CRATERS COPERNICUS, REINHOLD, MOON. *Apollo 12, NASA.*

25. CRATER TSIOLKOVSKY, MOON. *Apollo 15, NASA.*

26. HADLEY RILLE, MOON. *Apollo 15*, NASA.

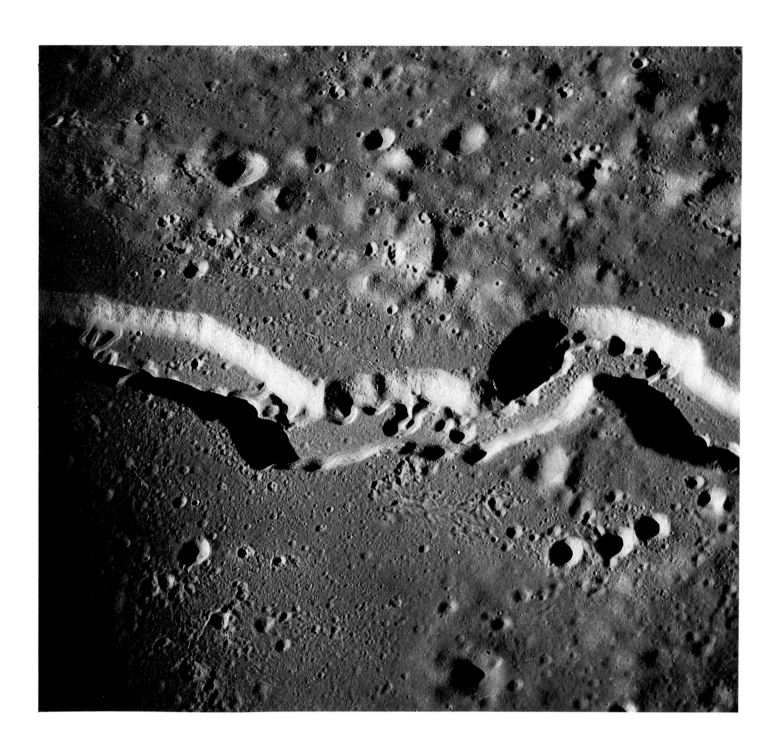

27. HADLEY RILLE, MOON. *Apollo* 15, NASA.

28. TAURUS-LITTROW AREA, MOON. *Eugene Cernan, NASA.*

29. TAURUS-LITTROW AREA, MOON. *Eugene Cernan, NASA.*

30. LUNAR MODULE OVER MOON. *Richard Gordon, NASA.*

31. EARTH OVER MOON. *Michael Collins, NASA.*

32. APOLLO 17 ASTRONAUT ON MOON. *Eugene Cernan, NASA.*

33. LUNAR ROVER, MOON. *Apollo 15, NASA.*

34. MOON ROCKS. NASA.

35. MOON ROCKS. NASA.

36. MOON ROCKS. NASA.

37. MOON ROCKS. NASA.

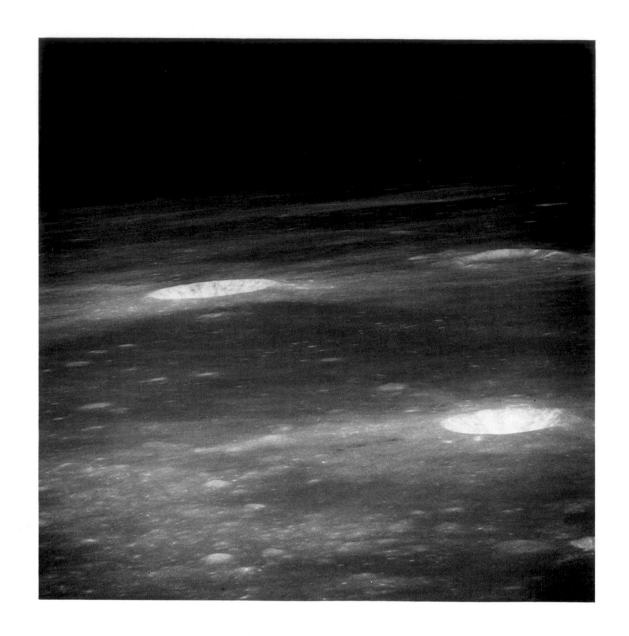

38. MOON. *Stuart Roosa, NASA.*

39. EARTH OVER MOON. *Apollo 14*, NASA.

40. SUN-FLASHED MOONSCAPE. *Apollo 17*, NASA.

41. SUN FROM SKYLAB. NASA.

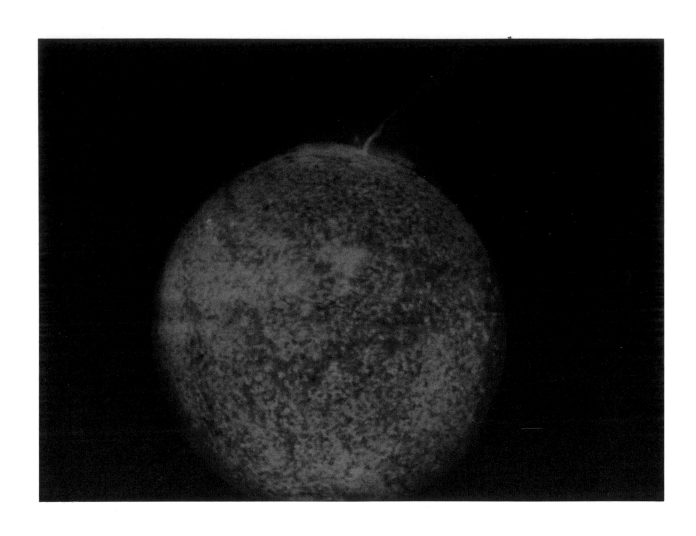

42. SUN FROM SKYLAB. *U.S. Naval Research Laboratory.*

43. TOTAL ECLIPSE OF THE SUN. *Patrick Wiggens, Hansen Planetarium.*

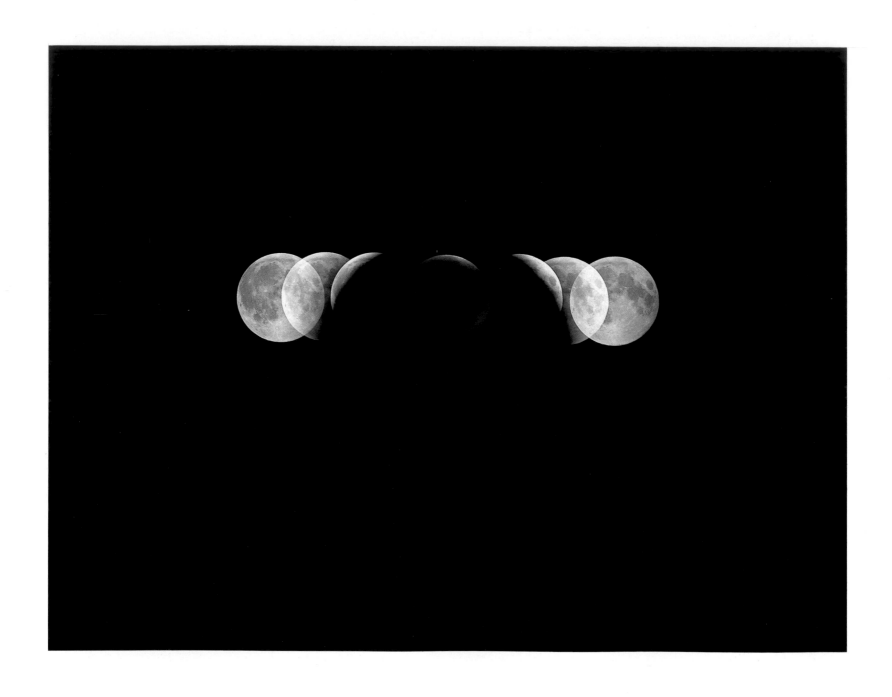

44. ECLIPSE OF THE MOON. *Akira Fujii.*

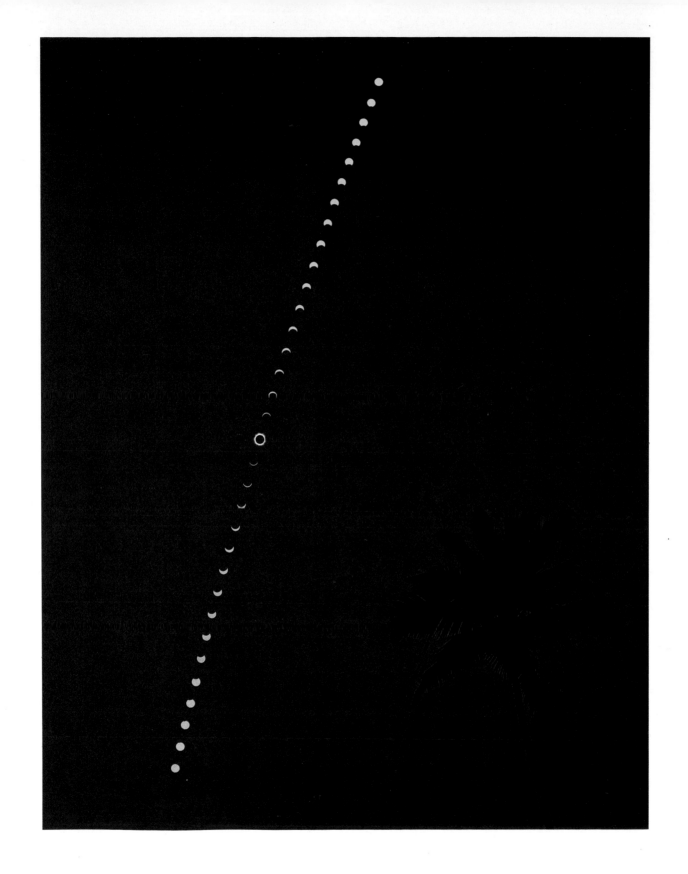

45. TOTAL ECLIPSE OF THE SUN. *Akira Fujii.*

46. ARCTIC AURORA. *John Richards.*

47. ARCTIC AURORA. *John Richards.*

48. MOON AND VENUS. *Johnny Horne.*

49. COMET WEST. *Lick Observatory.*

50. PLAIN OF GOLD, MARS. *Viking 1 lander*, NASA.

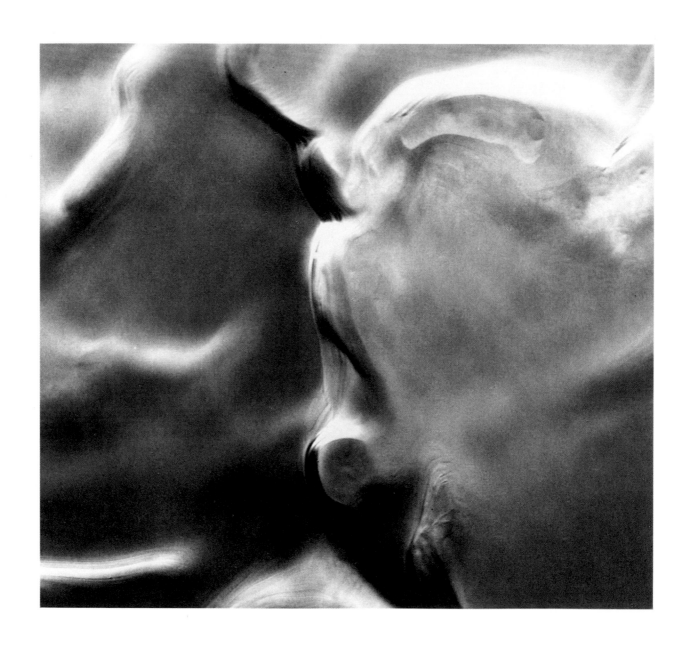

51. NORTH POLAR REGION, MARS. *Viking 2 orbiter, NASA.*

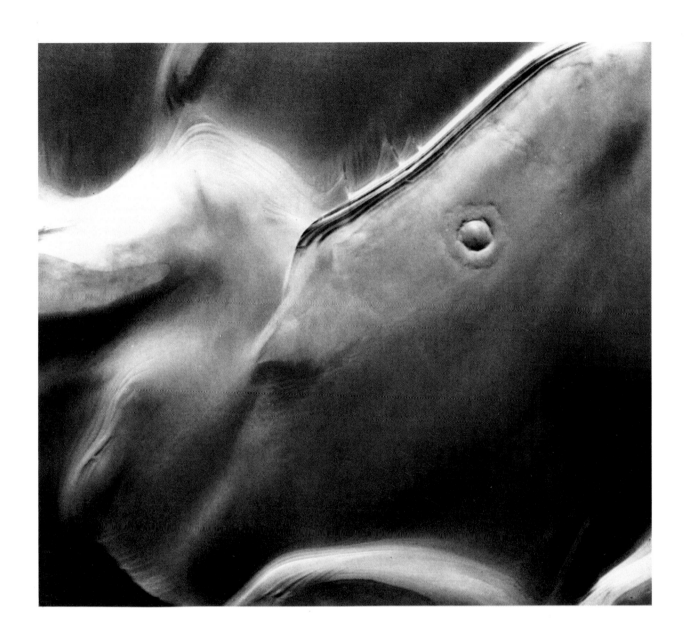

52. NORTH POLAR REGION, MARS. *Viking 2 orbiter, NASA.*

53. POLAR ICE CAP, MARS. *Viking 2 orbiter, NASA.*

54. POLAR ICE CAP, MARS. *Viking 2 orbiter,* NASA.

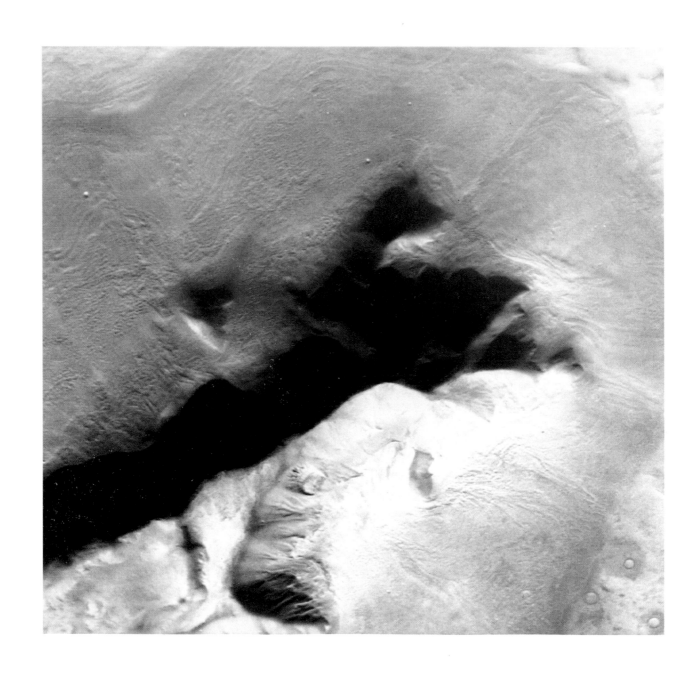

55. MOUNTAINS OF MARS. *Viking orbiter, NASA.*

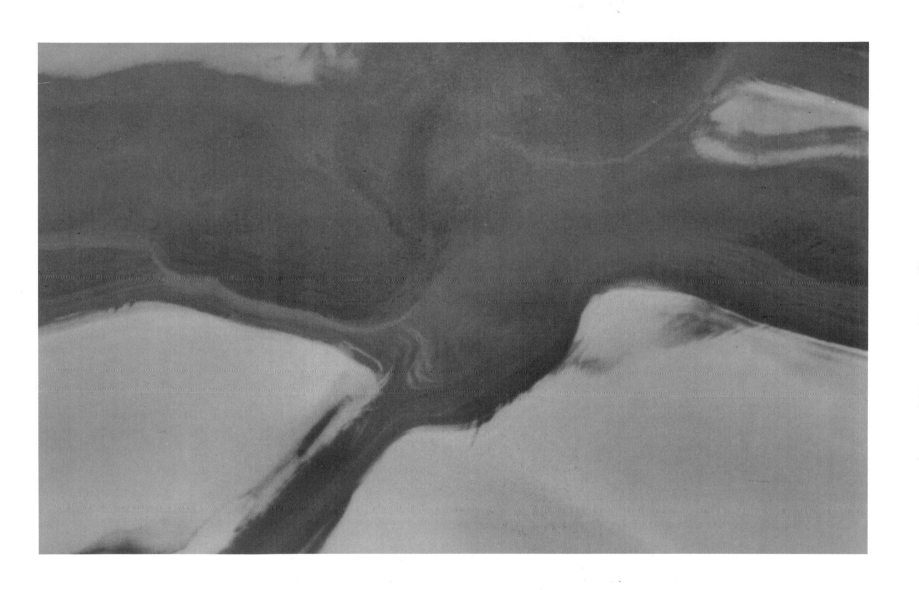

56. NORTH POLAR REGION, MARS. *Viking 2 orbiter*, NASA.

57. MARINER VALLEY, MARS. *Viking orbiter, NASA.*

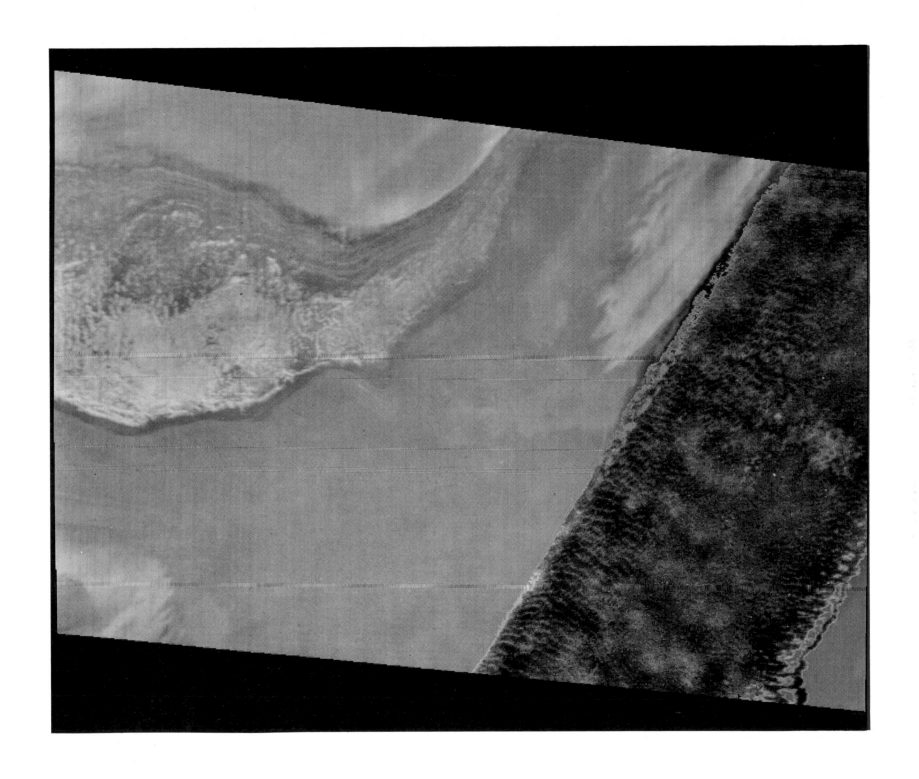

58. SAND DUNES AND SNOWFIELDS, MARS. *Viking 2 orbiter, NASA.*

59. IO, SATELLITE OF JUPITER. *Voyager, NASA.*

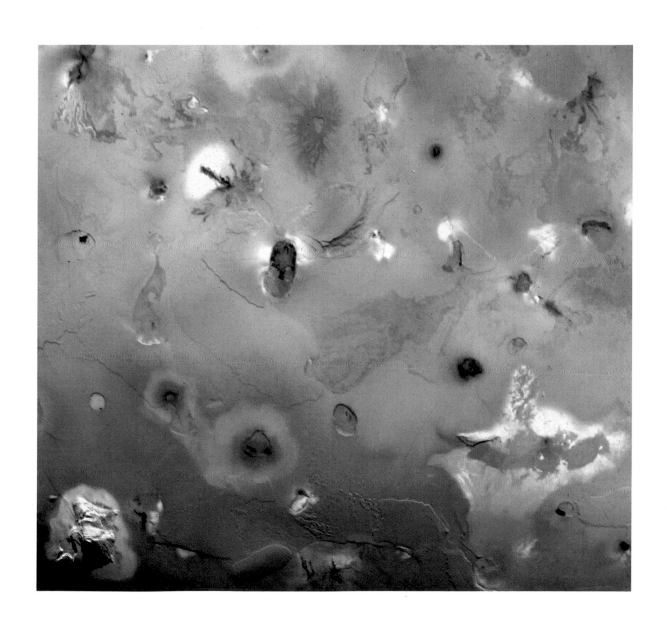

60. IO, SATELLITE OF JUPITER. *Voyager*, NASA.

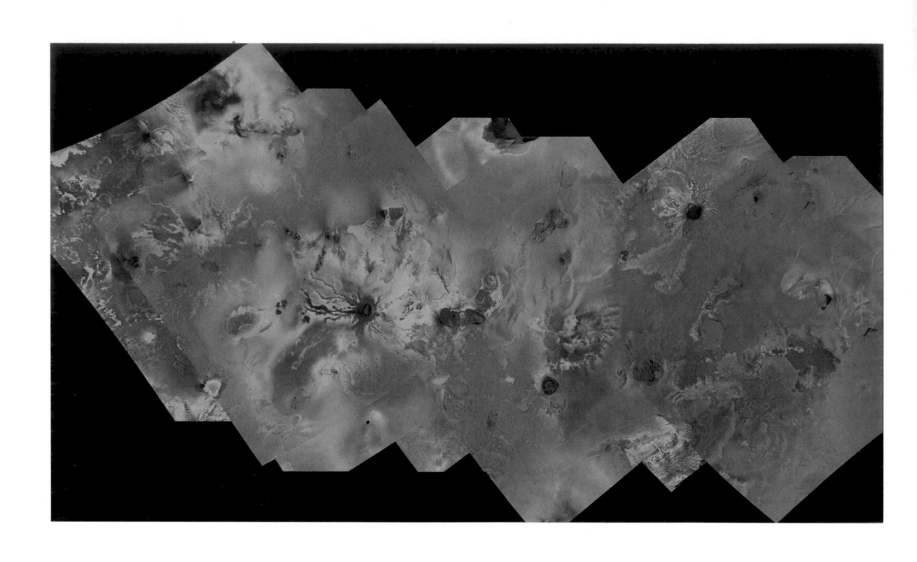

61. IO, SATELLITE OF JUPITER. *Voyager, NASA.*

62. KITT PEAK, ARIZONA. *Gary Ladd.*

63. ORION NEBULA. *Anglo-Australian Observatory.*

64. MONOCEROS NEBULA. *Palomar Observatory.*

65. GALAXY M104. *Kitt Peak National Observatory.*

66. GALAXY M51. *Kitt Peak National Observatory.*

67. GALAXY M81. *Mount Wilson and Las Campanas Observatories.*

68. GALAXY M83. *Mount Wilson and Las Campanas Observatories.*

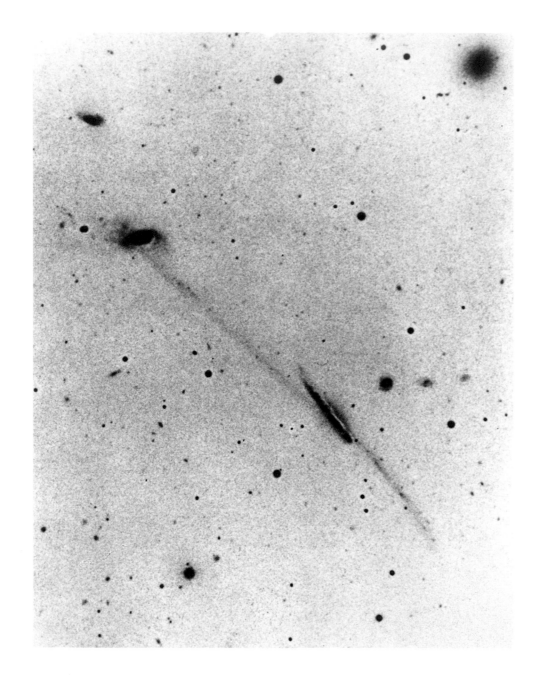

69. **INTERACTING GALAXIES.** *Mount Wilson and Las Campanas Observatories.*

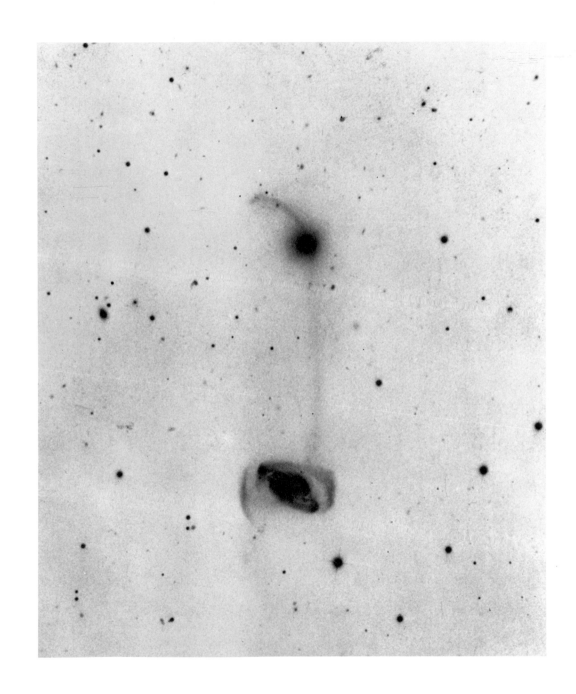

70. INTERACTING GALAXIES. *Mount Wilson and Las Campanas Observatories.*

71. VEIL NEBULA. *Mount Wilson and Las Campanas Observatories.*

72. TRIFID NEBULA. *Kitt Peak National Observatory.*

73. LARGE MAGELLANIC CLOUD. *European Southern Observatory.*

74. GALAXY M31. *Palomar Observatory.*

75. STAR TRAILS, SOUTHERN HEMISPHERE. *Douglas Kirkland.*

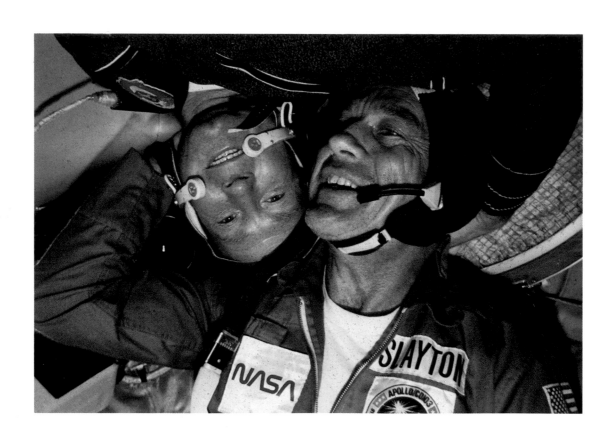

76. APOLLO ASTRONAUT AND SOYUZ COSMONAUT. NASA.

77. EARTH. *Apollo 11, NASA:*

78. COMET BENNETT. *Akira Fujii.*

About the Photographs

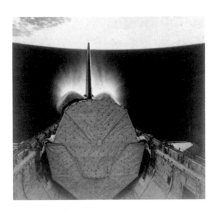

1. EARTH FROM SHUTTLE

IGNITION OF THE ENGINES of the space shuttle *Columbia*'s six-thousand-pound thrust orbital maneuvering system (OMS) created the bright glow visible in this view looking tailward from the shuttle's aft flight-deck station. The OMS engines are fired to raise or lower the shuttle's altitude in orbit and to permit reentry into Earth's atmosphere.

Here, *Columbia*'s cargo bay doors have been opened to space, exposing a canister that contains a communications satellite awaiting launch into orbit. Portions of *Columbia*'s wings appear at either side, and the horizon of the earth is at the top of the frame. In orbit, space shuttles spend most of their time "upside down," with the earth stretched out across the crew's overhead windows.

Taken November 11, 1982, on 70mm color-reversal film. *NASA Johnson Space Center*.

2. MARS

THE VIKING 2 SPACECRAFT took this image of Mars as it approached the red planet in August 1976. North is to the left. The prominent volcano is Ascraeus Mons, named for Ascrae, the birthplace of Hesiod. The plume extending westward from the slopes of the volcano is a water-ice cloud produced by winds blowing across the mountain peak. Dust clouds obscured much of the northern hemisphere this day, but Ascraeus Mons, sixty thousand feet high, was lofty enough to poke through the cloud cover. The enormous canyon stretching from center to right is Valles Marineris (see Photograph 57).

The 51,539 color and black-and-white photographs made by the twin *Viking* orbiters mapped 97 percent of the Martian surface at a resolution of one thousand feet. (For *Viking* orbiter images, see Photographs 51 to 58.) Each orbiter dispatched a lander to the surface; together the landers transmitted over 4,500 photographs. The *Viking* 1 lander, longest lived of the four probes, transmitted data from the surface of Mars for over three and a half years. (See Photograph 50 for a *Viking* lander view of Mars.) *NASA Jet Propulsion Laboratory*.

SATURN'S TINY SATELLITE Enceladus is only 310 miles in diameter. We would expect anything that small to have cooled off completely billions of years ago and to have been geologically inert ever since, as is Earth's moon. Instead, Enceladus looks upon close inspection geologically young and active. Many of its impact craters—scars suffered when the solar system was young and still full of interplanetary debris—have been erased by subsequent flooding of the surface. Some of this activity appears to have taken place as little as a hundred million years ago, very recently indeed by geological standards. One theory is that Enceladus pulsates due to gravitational interaction with other Saturnian satellites, and that it may fume with water volcanos analogous to the sulphur volcanos of Io (Photographs 59 to 61). No such volcanos were observed during *Voyager*'s brief encounter with Enceladus, but the satellite displays ridges that could have been created by rivers of flowing water. Its surface sheathed in ice, Enceladus is brighter than new-fallen snow. *NASA Jet Propulsion Laboratory.*

3. ENCELADUS

SATURN, ITS RINGS, and two of its satellites are seen at a range of eight million miles in this *Voyager 1* photograph, taken November 3, 1980. The edge of Saturn's cloud-top surface can be seen through the divisions in the ring system. An observer floating high in the clouds of Saturn would see a blue sky overhead; traces of that blue can be seen along the edge of the planet. The satellites are Tethys, above, and Dione. The dark spot at the lower left is Tethys' shadow. *NASA Jet Propulsion Laboratory.*

4. SATURN AND SATELLITES

THE FAR SIDE OF SATURN was photographed by the *Voyager 1* spacecraft following its passage through the Saturn system in November, 1980. For scale, consider that the diameter of the rings is about equal to the distance from Earth to the moon.

Saturn was the last hurrah for *Voyager 1*. The velocity imparted to the spacecraft during its passage near the giant planets Jupiter and Saturn hurled it on a trajectory leading out of the solar system and into interstellar space. Adrift in the Milky Way, *Voyager* can be expected to last for over a billion years, making it one of the most nearly permanent objects ever built by human hands. *NASA Jet Propulsion Laboratory.*

5. FAR SIDE OF SATURN

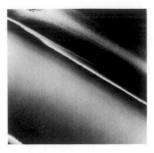

6. HORIZON OF TITAN

THE THICK ATMOSPHERE of Saturn's satellite Titan was photographed by the *Voyager* spacecraft when Titan stood between *Voyager* and the sun; the colors of the resulting backlit portrait have been enhanced by computer. Though Titan is about the same size and density as Jupiter's large satellites Ganymede (Photographs 8 and 9) and Callisto, only Titan retains a dense atmosphere; it is ten times thicker than Earth's, and, like Earth's, is composed predominantly of nitrogen. Hydrocarbons are present in abundance. Since hydrocarbons are the building blocks of life on Earth, Titan, despite its cold climate (minus 290 degrees Fahrenheit), might conceivably be an abode of extraterrestrial life. *NASA Jet Propulsion Laboratory.*

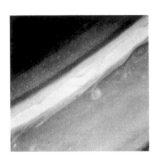

7. SURFACE OF SATURN

LIKE JUPITER, Saturn is swathed in a thick envelope of clouds. Both planets rotate once every ten hours, and in both, atmospheric circulation patterns have arranged the visible surface clouds into a system of bands paralleling the equator. Saturn, however, is less massive and less dense than Jupiter, and its surface features differ from those of Jupiter. The colors of the clouds—thought, like Jupiter's, to be caused by the presence of complex organic molecules, though just which molecules is uncertain—are more muted than Jupiter's. The wind speeds on the surface of Saturn are higher, attaining velocities of a thousand miles per hour at the equator.

The *Voyager 2* image of Saturn's mid-northern latitudes, taken at a range of 5.8 million miles, shows eddies and knots in the belts as small as fifty-six miles in diameter. *NASA Jet Propulsion Laboratory.*

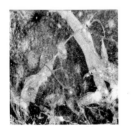

8, 9. GANYMEDE

JUPITER'S SATELLITE GANYMEDE resembles a frozen sun: it is made of about the same mixture of elements with which the sun began. Jupiter's inner satellites Io and Europa, however, are lacking in lighter elements. The boiling away of their volatiles is ascribed to the infant Jupiter, which was thought to have glowed so hotly in its early days that the solar system looked like a double star.

The grooved face of Ganymede is a mystery. The grooves are hundreds of yards deep and stretch for hundreds of miles, covering 60 percent of the satellite's surface. One explanation is that they are wrinkles created by pressure in the crust. Another is that the grooves were cut by liquid water— brine, perhaps—that flowed on Ganymede three billion years ago. Like its sister Jovian satellite Callisto, Ganymede is covered with ice—an anatomy that gives both moons the shimmering, evanescent appearance of crystal balls. Geological convulsions in Ganymede might have created a network of rivers that ran just beneath the ice. *NASA Jet Propulsion Laboratory.*

THESE HIGH-RESOLUTION *Voyager* spacecraft photographs show the clouds of Jupiter's upper atmosphere in the vicinity of the Great Red Spot (Photograph 12). Some of the knots and eddies of Jupiter's atmosphere can change shape rapidly, prodded by 200-mile-per-hour winds and by upwellings of gas from as far as six hundred miles down. Yet others manage to maintain their identity for decades. The Great Red Spot, the largest cyclone on the surface of Jupiter, has been swirling away for some three hundred years. Scientists who study Jovian meteorology attribute the longevity of the larger features in part to the sluggishness of the cold environment: Jupiter receives only 4 percent as much solar heat as the earth, and the temperature at the cloud tops is a chilly minus 200 degrees Fahrenheit. *NASA Jet Propulsion Laboratory.*

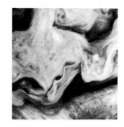

10, 11. SURFACE OF JUPITER

THIS PHOTOGRAPH of the giant planet Jupiter and two of its satellites, Io, left, and Europa, is a composite of three filtered black-and-white images transmitted in succession by *Voyager* 1 as it approached the Jovian system in February 1979. The range was 12.4 million miles. The two satellites are each about 2,000 miles in diameter. The smallest features that can be seen on the planet's face are about 250 miles in diameter.

Jupiter is more than twice as massive as all the sun's other planets combined. Its gravity, 2.4 times that of Earth, has allowed Jupiter to retain the light gases that must have been present at the creation of all the planets, but that were lost by the smaller planets like Earth. Consequently, Jupiter today is still composed chiefly of the two most abundant elements in the universe, hydrogen and helium. Its interior is thought to be composed of an outer sheath of gases, enveloping a ball of liquid metallic hydrogen that in turn contains a small, solid core.

What we see on the surface are clouds, arranged into latitudinal bands that are broken by roiling eddies. The largest of these eddies, the Great Red Spot, seen here behind Io, is substantially larger than Earth. *NASA Jet Propulsion Laboratory.*

12. JUPITER AND SATELLITES

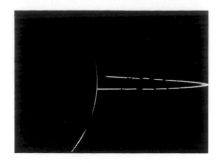

13. JUPITER'S RING

17. JUPITER'S RING

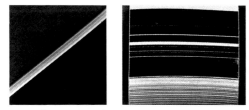

14, 16. SATURN'S RINGS

15. SATURN'S RINGS

JUPITER'S RING was discovered in a photograph made by the *Voyager 1* spacecraft on March 4, 1979, bringing to three the number of planets known to have rings: Jupiter and Saturn, and the remote planet Uranus, whose ring system was found during observations of an occultation—an eclipse—of a star by Uranus in 1977.

The existence of a Jovian ring had been predicted by theorists, and the computers aboard *Voyager 1* were programmed to search for it by making long-exposure photos from the dark side of the planet. When *Voyager 2* arrived at Jupiter four months later, it imaged the ring system more extensively, taking two wide-angle and four narrow-angle photographs that were pieced together on Earth to create the black-and-white mosaic of Photograph 13. The interruptions are intervals between the photographs, not gaps in the ring itself; the gap nearest Jupiter, however, was created by the planet's own shadow. Photograph 13 was taken from a range of just under a billion miles, as *Voyager* sped away from Jupiter on its way toward Saturn.

Photograph 17 combines *Voyager 2* images made through orange and violet filters. Whipping through Jupiter's gravitational well at a velocity of over fifty thousand miles per hour, the spacecraft moved so far between the two successive exposures that the images of Jupiter were offset, creating the illusion of two Jovian horizons in contrasting colors.

Voyager's studies of the Jovian rings established that they were composed entirely of tiny particles of dust, unlike Saturn's rings (Photographs 4, 5, 14, 15), which have particles of snowball size and larger. Such tiny particles cannot long survive in Jupiter's ring; slowed by collisions with other particles in the Jovian environment, they must eventually fall into the planet. Therefore something must be replenishing the rings. Conceivably material ejected by the volcanoes of Jupiter's satellite Io do the job. (Photographs 12, 59 to 61). *NASA Jet Propulsion Laboratory.*

THESE THREE PERSPECTIVES on Saturn's rings were obtained by cameras aboard the *Voyager* spacecraft. Photograph 14 shows the rings almost edge-on and suggests something of their considerable complexity. Astronomers observing Saturn from Earth had known for centuries that there were at least three rings, and had wondered whether there might not be more. *Voyager* in fact found over nine hundred rings. The disposition of particles in the rings and the spacing of the intervals that separate them is thought to result from gravitational resonances between the ring particles and Saturn's satellites: the Saturn system is a Newtonian orchestra, and, thanks to the rings, we can read its music.

Photographs 15 and 16 employ computer-generated false colors to enhance contrasts between the rings. Photograph 15 was taken by *Voyager 1* from the shadowed side of the rings, only ten hours prior to the spacecraft's closest encounter with Saturn. Lit from the back, the rings display brightness patterns opposite to those of the sunlit side. The Cassini Division, so dark when seen from Earth that it looks like empty space, is bright —it's the thin white line crossing the photograph at top and bottom— and the B ring, the broad causeway here painted red by the computer, looks dark. (See also Photograph 5.)

Photograph 16 is a high-resolution reconstruction from data gathered by a photopolarimeter aboard *Voyager 2*. This instrument charted the opacity of the rings by measuring the brightness of a star as the rings passed in front of it. The resulting image centers on the Encke Division, a gap in the outer regions of the A ring. The red lines crossing at center are part of a small ringlet that inhabits the Encke Division. Resolution is as fine as 1.2 miles.

Saturn's is the most spectacular, but not the only, ring system in the solar system. Jupiter, too, has a ring (Photograph 17), as does Uranus, target of a *Voyager 2* encounter in 1986. NASA *Jet Propulsion Laboratory*.

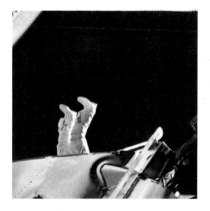

18. APOLLO 9 SPACEWALK

ASTRONAUT RUSSELL SCHWEICKART emerges feet first from the *Apollo 9* lunar module to begin a forty-seven-minute excursion into space. The ten-day Earth-orbital mission was launched March 3, 1969, to test equipment that would be employed four months later on the first manned moon landing. Schweickart wore a self-contained backpack of the kind that was to supply air to *Apollo 11* astronauts Neil Armstrong and Edwin Aldrin on the moon. While outside the craft, Schweickart made his way along a set of handrails from the lunar module to the command module, to test whether astronauts in lunar orbit could gain entry to the command module this way, in case a technical problem prevented their docking with it.

Schweickart's spacewalk was photographed by command-module pilot David Scott, who stood in an open hatch, his upper body immersed in space (see Photograph 22). The scheduled procedures were delayed when Scott's camera jammed. "Give me five minutes to try and fix the camera," Scott said to Schweickhart. The result, Schweickart recalled, was that "I had about five minutes in which I had nothing to do. Except to take that time to think about what I was doing . . . and look down at the earth."

The spacecraft was approaching the West Coast of the United States as Schweickart floated in space, free for once from the pressure of his duties. It was "an absolutely spectacular sight," he recalled. "When you're going along at seventeen thousand miles an hour with this incredible, spectacular panorama below you—and absolute, total silence—you can't imagine how beautiful it is. . . . I completely lost my identity as an American astronaut. I felt a part of everyone and everything sweeping past me below."

Photograph by David Scott. NASA *Johnson Space Center*.

19. SECOND MAN ON MOON

THIS PORTRAIT OF EDWIN "BUZZ" ALDRIN, the second man to set foot on the moon, was taken by Neil Armstrong, who preceded him. Armstrong's image is reflected in the gold-plated visor of Aldrin's helmet, along with their landing craft, the lunar excursion module, or LM. Armstrong began taking photographs almost from the moment he stepped out onto the lunar surface, even postponing the critical mission of collecting a lunar soil sample while he took panoramic snapshots along the horizon. "It has a stark beauty all its own," he radioed back to Earth.

Aldrin stepped out of the LM and onto the lunar surface a few minutes later. His first words were, "Beautiful! Beautiful!"

"Magnificent sight down here," Armstrong replied. Upon their return, the *Apollo* 11 crew members asked NASA to schedule fifteen or twenty minutes of free time for future moonwalkers, so they could simply pause and enjoy the sensation of being on the moon.

The descent of Armstrong and Aldrin from lunar orbit to the surface had been marked by two emergencies. At one point the on-board computer in the LM signaled a data overload. A ground controller, Steve Bales, instantly advised that the problem was not serious and cleared the astronauts to continue their descent—a decisive act for which he later was awarded the Presidential Medal of Freedom. Armstrong, standing in a safety harness at the controls of the LM, was distracted by the computer alarm and lost sight of landmarks he had planned to use to find his way to the landing site. When he regained his bearings he found that the automatic landing system was taking them into a boulder field. He assumed manual control—"I was being absolutely adamant about my right to be wishy-washy about where I was going to land," he said later—and kept the LM aloft until they had cleared the boulders and reached a clear area "about the size of a big house lot." The two touched down with less than thirty seconds' worth of fuel remaining. Neither showed any noticeable sign of excitement during the descent, but Aldrin admits that he urinated moments after setting foot on the moon. "Neil might have been the first man to step on the moon," he recalled in his memoirs, "but I was the first to pee in his pants on the moon."

Armstrong and Aldrin spent two hours and forty minutes taking photographs and deploying scientific experiments on the lunar surface. They left olive branches to symbolize world peace, medallions and patches honoring three American and two Soviet space explorers killed in the line of duty, and a plaque inscribed with the words, "Here men from the planet Earth first set foot upon the Moon July 1969, A.D. We came in peace for all mankind." They responded to a speech by the President of the United States, and they gathered soil samples. Then they returned to the LM, repressurized it, took off their helmets, and found that the lunar soil had filled the cabin with an odor like that of wet ashes. They slept fitfully—it was cold, and Armstrong's sleeping sling placed him in a position where light from Earth shone through a telescope directly into his eyes—awakened, secured their gear, blasted off from the moon and joined the *Apollo 11* command module in lunar orbit.

Back on Earth, after the official celebrations were over, the first men to walk on the moon slowly withdrew from public view. Armstrong took a teaching job and refused requests for interviews. Aldrin was hospitalized for chronic depression. The moon landing had played to mixed reviews, and Armstrong and Aldrin were once pelted with tomatoes when they visited a college campus to accept an award.

The unpopularity of the Apollo project has been blamed on the war in Vietnam and on the bland, all-American image NASA tailored for the astronauts. Doubtless these were contributing factors, but it may have been due as well to the ambivalence with which societies tend to regard feats of exploration. Marco Polo wound up in jail when he returned from his adventures, Columbus fell into disrepute, and the ancient Chinese destroyed the ships and logbooks of their greatest explorers.

Photographed by Neil Armstrong, July 20, 1969, on 70mm color-reversal film, ASA 64. NASA *Johnson Space Center*.

ASTRONAUT JOSEPH KERWIN exercises in weightlessness aboard *Skylab*, the first American space station. This photograph was taken from a live television image transmitted by a camera in the forward compartment of the Skylab Orbital Workshop, on June 1, 1973, during the twenty-eight-day Skylab 2 mission.

While the two-hundred-thousand-pound *Skylab* orbited Earth at an altitude of two hundred seventy miles, the astronauts aboard carried out a variety of scientific missions, among them extensive observations of the sun at wavelengths not visible from the surface of Earth. For two of the resulting portraits of the sun, see Photos 41 and 42. NASA *Johnson Space Center*.

20. ASTRONAUT

ASTRONAUT BRUCE MCCANDLESS became the first human satellite when he drifted untethered in space 170 miles above the earth on February 7, 1984. To make his excursion, McCandless donned a spacesuit, entered the cargo bay of the space shuttle *Challenger*, fitted himself to an aluminum manned maneuvering unit (MMU) and fired tiny nitrogen-gas thrusters to leave the shuttle behind. His velocity was seventeen thousand miles per hour relative to the surface of the earth, but never more than one mile per hour relative to *Challenger*.

It was the first space mission for McCandless, forty-six, a captain in the Navy and an ardent environmentalist. It culminated eighteen years of

21. UNTETHERED SPACEWALK

astronaut training and ten years spent developing the MMU backpack. "It really is beautiful," he said of his unimpeded view of Cape Canaveral, Florida, where the shuttle had been launched four days earlier. He began his spacewalk over the Pacific Ocean, and was above Africa by the time he returned to the shuttle's cargo bay.

The maneuvering system resembles a chair but has no seat, since it is to be used only in weightlessness. Its thrusters—one set of twelve plus a backup set for safety—are operated by hand controls. A camera is mounted on the boom that extends above the astronaut's right shoulder. The unit was designed to enable astronauts to repair satellites and perform other functions in space.

Later the same morning, McCandless was joined on his free-floating excursion by Robert Stewart. The two spent a total of six hours outside the shuttle.

Photograph by shuttle commander Vance Brand. NASA *Johnson Space Center.*

22. APOLLO IN EARTH ORBIT

DAVID SCOTT poked his head into space to take snapshots of Russell Schweickart's spacewalk (Photograph 18), while Schweickart in turn made this photograph of Scott. The dual space excursions took place during the *Apollo* 9 Earth orbital mission. The third member of the crew, commander James McDivitt, remained inside, overseeing the operation of the spacecraft. The Pacific Ocean is in the background.

Photo by Russell Schweickart. NASA *Johnson Space Center.*

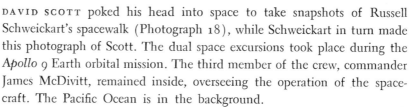

23. APOLLO OVER MOON

THE APOLLO COMMAND MODULE, polished to a mirror finish to reflect the heat of the sun, is seen face-on in this view from the lunar module in orbit above the moon. The spacecraft's Earth-communications antenna sprouts like a boutonniere at the lower right; its hatch windows can be seen at the eleven and one o'clock positions. Twelve feet, ten inches in diameter and weighing 12,500 pounds, the command module afforded three astronauts a "habitable volume" of 210 cubic feet—about the size of a walk-in clothes closet—during voyages to and from the moon.

This photo was taken during the *Apollo* 10 mission, when three astronauts orbited the moon at altitudes as low as forty-seven thousand feet, detached the lunar module, flew it, and docked it with the command module in a final test of the procedures to be employed in the first manned moon landing less than two months later. Below the command module is a heavily cratered region on the far side of the moon, about 175 miles east of Smyth's Sea, one of the most easterly bits of moonscape visible from Earth. The sun was almost directly overhead. The photo was made on 70mm color-reversal film with a 250mm lens. *NASA Johnson Space Center.*

THE CRATERS of the moon vary considerably in age. Most were formed billions of years ago, when bombardment of planets and their satellites by debris from space was much more common than today. But some craters are younger, indicating that epochs of meteor bombardment have recurred more recently in the history of the solar system. Radiation dating of impact craters on Earth suggests that meteor storms may strike at periodic intervals of roughly every twenty-six to thirty-three million years, and that climatic changes triggered by these bombardments could have touched off episodes of mass extinction like the one sixty-five million years ago in which the dinosaurs perished. Since meteor showers that hit the Earth ought to have hit our neighbor the moon as well, data on the precise ages of large numbers of lunar craters could confirm or deny the theory that meteor showers are periodic.

Copernicus, one of the youngest and most spectacular craters on the near side of the moon, lies toward the horizon in Photo 24, taken from lunar orbit during the Apollo 12 mission. Bright rays of ejecta radiate outward from Copernicus halfway across the face of the moon; they can be seen easily from Earth through binoculars or a small telescope. The fact that the rays spread uninterruptedly across other lunar features testifies to the relatively low age of Copernicus, estimated at nine hundred million years.

Fifty-five miles in diameter and eleven thousand four hundred feet deep, Copernicus covers an area equal to that of Belgium. The craters in the foreground are Reinhold A and B. The crater at the one o'clock position, nearer Copernicus, Fauth, is thirty-six hundred feet deep.

Photo 25, taken on the third lunar orbit of the Apollo 15 mission, shows the larger and older crater Tsiolkovsky, home to one of only two lava-filled basins to be found on the far side of the moon. All the other lava basins are on the near side. Lava is released by upwelling from beneath the crust, so scientists hypothesize that the lunar crust must be thicker on the far than on the near side. Tsiolkovsky's central mountain is characteristic of large impact craters—Copernicus has one too—and results from the dynamics of the high-speed impact of the meteor that formed the crater. The diameter of Tsiolkovsky is one hundred eighteen miles, more than twice that of mighty Copernicus. *NASA Johnson Space Center.*

24. COPERNICUS AND REINHOLD

25. TSIOLKOVSKY

36. MOON ROCKS

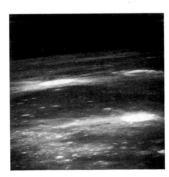

37. MOON ROCKS

38. MOON

oceans, not of water but of molten rock—and some lighter-colored rocks found in the lunar highlands resemble such terrestrial rocks as norite, anorthosite, and gabbro.

But moon rocks can also be quite different from those of Earth. Since the moon lacks water to dissolve minerals, structures like the crystals evident in Photographs 34 and 35 have remained unaltered for billions of years. Three minerals never before seen on Earth were found in moon rocks: armalcolite (named for the *Apollo 11* astronauts, *Armstrong, Aldrin* and *Collins*), pyroxferroite (named for pyroxene and iron), and tranquillityite (named for Tranquillity Base, where it was first encountered). Moreover, the chemical composition of similar rocks varies with their location on the moon. Solidified lava collected at the *Apollo 11* and *17* landing sites are rich in titanium (the black shards clearly visible in Photograph 37), while outwardly identical rocks found at the *Apollo 12* and *15* sites are poor in titanium.

Were the moon as simple as some researchers thought, we might have solved most of its mysteries by now. Instead, the moon turns out to be complex, and to have a lot left to teach us. The bulk of lunar rocks and soil gathered by the Apollo project remain in Houston, patiently awaiting further study as theory and technology improve. After all, it may be a long time before anyone goes to the moon again. *NASA Johnson Space Center.*

THREE CRATERS of the Lansberg group stand out in this photograph taken by astronaut Stuart Roosa from the *Apollo 14* command module in lunar orbit. Lunar soil excavated by meteors that hit the moon and produced the Lansberg craters is lighter in color than the soil of the lunar surface because, unlike the surface, it has not yet endured aeons of exposure to "weathering" by micrometeorites and the solar wind. Such weathering has roughened and darkened old lunar soil. The photo was made using 70mm black-and-white film and an 80mm lens, looking aft from the command module as it approached a point directly above the *Apollo 14* landing site. It was there that an insouciant Alan Shepard, taking a break from his scheduled activities, hit a golf ball with a six-iron and sent it soaring "miles and miles" across the moon. *NASA Johnson Space Center.*

AS APOLLO 14 ASTRONAUTS Alan Shepard, Stuart Roosa, and Edgar Mitchell made a last swing around the far side of the moon in 1971, they photographed the earth, their destination, as it rose over the lunar horizon. The craters in the foreground, Firsov and Lobachevsky, lie on the far side of the moon. Unmanned Soviet space probes were the first to photograph the far side of the moon, and, consequently, maps of the far side are peppered with Russian names, though there are also far-side craters named for Thomas Edison, Jules Verne, and the mystic Giordano Bruno, who was burned at the stake in 1600 for insisting, among other heresies, that the universe contained many inhabited planets.

Earth and the moon display complementary phases as viewed from each other; when the moon appears as a crescent from Earth, Earth is nearly full as seen from the moon. Since the earth was a crescent when this photograph was taken, the earthward side of the moon was almost full, and the far side, therefore, was dark. The resulting gloom of lunar twilight lends a brooding quality to this portrait of Firsov and Lobachevsky. *NASA Johnson Space Center.*

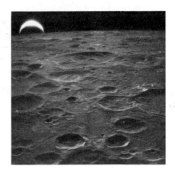

39. EARTH OVER MOON

THE CAMERAS EMPLOYED by the Apollo astronauts sometimes failed, under exposure to the cold vacuum of space and to the general rough-and-tumble of exploratory expeditions. A camera jammed during an Apollo 9 spacewalk; during the Apollo 12 mission on the moon a camera back sprang open, flooding the film with light, and another film magazine was inadvertently left behind on the moon. But as artists and scientists know, the results of accidents can be as interesting as the results of planning. In this case, light leaking onto exposed film in a Hasselblad magazine released a torrent of dyes latent in the emulsion, painting the lunar landscape in psychedelic colors that it last possessed, if ever, in the days when the solar system was still being formed and meteorites were raining down on a molten lunar surface. The photograph was taken in December 1972, during the Apollo 17 exploration of the foothills of the Taurus Mountains—a site located at the right edge of the right eye of the "Man in the Moon." *NASA Johnson Space Center.*

40. MOONSCAPE

41, 42. SUN FROM SKYLAB

THESE TWO IMAGES of the sun were taken in ultraviolet light, at wavelengths that Earth's atmosphere blocks from reaching the surface, through telescopes aboard the *Skylab* space station. They show two giant solar prominences, tongues of gas arching up from the turbulent solar surface. Colors have been added to approximate the color radiated by hydrogen, the most abundant element in the sun. The scale is large; the prominence in Photograph 42, for instance, is taller than the distance from Earth to the moon. *Naval Research Laboratory; NASA Johnson Space Center.*

43. TOTAL ECLIPSE

THE DIAMETER OF THE SUN is four hundred times that of the moon, but as luck would have it, the sun is four hundred times further away. As a result of this coincidence, we are treated to the spectacle of our planet's satellite neatly blocking out the disk of our mother star.

A total solar eclipse is quite a sight: the sun dwindles to a slim crescent, the sky grows dark, and the air turns cold; the moon's shadow comes sweeping across the landscape at two thousand miles per hour; darkness descends and the stars come out, while off in the distance the world beyond the shadow glows in the color of sterling silver. One's appreciation for the sun is enhanced upon seeing its light so suddenly extinguished.

The temporary loss of the sun is compensated for, however, by the momentary glimpse an eclipse affords of the sun's outer atmosphere. The glowing ruby-red prominences (see Photographs 41 and 42) come into view and, extending far beyond them, the pearlescent filaments of the corona, the thin outer atmosphere of the sun, are arrayed along delicate tendrils marshaled by lines of magnetic force.

At the onset and the end of a solar eclipse, sunlight shining through valleys on the edge of the moon creates the "diamond-ring" effect. This photograph of the diamond ring was taken on February 16, 1980, at the Tsavo East game reserve in Kenya, by Patrick Wiggins of the Hansen Planetarium in Salt Lake City, Utah. Mr. Wiggins used a commercially available five-inch Schmidt Cassegrain telescope with an $f/10$ optical system shortened by use of a corrector lens to $f/5$, to widen the field. He used ASA 200 transparency film. *Hansen Planetarium, Patrick Wiggins.*

THESE TWO MULTIPLE-EXPOSURE photographs show eclipses of the moon (Photograph 44) and of the sun (Photograph 45). The lunar-eclipse sequence clearly reveals the circular shape of the earth's shadow, regarded by ancient Greek astronomers as evidence that the earth is a sphere. The circular form eclipsing the sun is the moon.

Akira Fujii photographed the lunar eclipse on December 30, 1982, the solar eclipse on February 16, 1980. The solar eclipse is the same one photographed in Africa by Patrick Wiggins in Photograph 43; Mr. Fujii observed it two and a half hours later, in India. *Akira Fujii.*

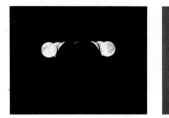 

44. ECLIPSE OF MOON　45. TOTAL ECLIPSE

AURORAE ARE TOUCHED OFF by storms on the sun. Solar flares send charged particles pouring out into space, and when the particles reach Earth they disrupt its magnetic field. Electrons spiral down toward the north and south magnetic poles, strike the upper atmosphere, and pump energy into atmospheric atoms, which then shake off the excess energy by emitting it as photons of light. The result is the glow of an aurora.

Aurorae reach their maximum intensity at about twenty-two degrees from each magnetic pole, and so are best seen in far northern and far southern latitudes. These displays were photographed at 68° north latitude in the Brooks Range in Alaska in January (Photograph 46) and December (Photograph 47), 1979, by John L. Richards, a meteorologist serving as a weather observer at a remote airfield north of Howard Pass. Mr. Richards employed 35mm ASA 200 film at $f/1.4$ with an exposure time of approximately six seconds.

The green tint of the aurora is produced largely by the excitement of nitrogen molecules high in the upper atmosphere. Compression of streams of electrons by the earth's magnetic field resulted in the draperylike sheets of light. In Photograph 46, the mountains are lit by a first-quarter moon, and the stars of Orion may be seen to the right, shimmering through the filmy aurora. The spidery blue patches at the base of Photograph 47 were produced by static electricity discharged when the film was rewound. Mr. Richards notes that humidity was low, the temperature minus 35 degrees Fahrenheit. *John L. Richards.*

46. ARCTIC AURORA

47. ARCTIC AURORA

THE MOON AND THE PLANET VENUS are seen here a few hours after the moon had passed in front of Venus, blocking the planet from view. Occultations of Venus by the moon are fairly rare. They always involve a crescent moon, since Venus never strays far from the sun in the sky. The photograph was taken on August 6, 1980, by Johnny Horne, an amateur astronomer and professional photographer, from his backyard observatory in Stedman, North Carolina. Mr. Horne exposed ASA 400 color-transparency film for ten seconds at the $f/4$ Newtonian focus of his 12.5-inch Cassegrain telescope. *Johnny Horne.*

48. MOON AND VENUS

49. COMET WEST

COMETS ARE INSUBSTANTIAL CHUNKS of ice and soil: "dirty snow-balls," astronomers call them. They are thought to originate in a vast cloud that surrounds the solar system, stretching as much as halfway to the nearest star and composed of scraps left over from the formation of the solar system. Perturbations produced in the cloud by the interaction of the drifting "snowballs" with the outer planets, passing stars, or with each other occasionally send one of them tumbling down toward the sun. Warmed by sunlight and blasted by the solar wind, which consists of charged particles streaming out from the sun, the comet sheds gas and dust, producing its characteristic tail. The nucleus of a typical comet measures only a few miles in diameter. The gas and dust escaping from the nucleus are so luminous that stars can be seen through the tail. The tail can stretch for tens of millions of miles, and its ghostly glow makes a major comet one of the most spectacular sights in the sky.

Comets do not streak across the sky like meteors; their motion against the background stars is evident only through a telescope. The tail gives them the appearance of great speed, but it simply points away from the sun, and has little to do with velocity.

This photograph, taken by astronomers at Lick Observatory in California on March 5, 1976, is of Comet West (1975n), one of the brightest comets of the twentieth century. Discovered by Richard West, a Danish astronomer at the European Southern Observatory in Geneva, Switzerland, it increased in brightness as it approached the sun until it could be discerned in broad daylight. When the photograph was taken it had whipped round the sun and was on its way back to the outer solar system. It is not expected to return for another several million years. Its brightness exceeded even that of Comet Bennett (Photograph 78). *Lick Observatory, University of California.*

50. PLAIN OF GOLD, MARS

THE VIKING 1 LANDER took this photograph early one summer morning on Chryse Planitia (Plain of Gold), in the northern hemisphere of Mars. A low-slung craft not much larger than a sidecar motorcycle, the lander "saw" Mars from a perspective something like that of a man sitting cross-legged on the sand. The dunes have been sculpted by Martian winds, which reached velocities of sixty miles per hour at the site, kicking up dust and sending small stones scurrying. *Viking* 1 endured several major windstorms during the three Martian years (six Earth years) that it transmitted data back to Earth. Its instruments confirmed that the climate was chilly (minus 120 degrees Fahrenheit just before dawn, minus 20 degrees by early afternoon) and the air thin (about one one-hundredth of that of Earth at sea level). Analysis of Martian soil dug up by the lander's mechanical arm indicated that it is an iron-rich clay, confirming the hypothesis that the red color of Mars comes from iron oxide, or rust. Soil samples were scooped up, dropped into three miniature automated laboratories atop the lander, and tested for signs of life, with ambiguous results. The Viking biology team concluded that they "do not permit any final conclusion about the presence of life on Mars."

The Viking landing sites do not necessarily represent typical Martian landscapes. To minimize the risk of crashing the spacecraft, bland, level deserts were selected, rather than the more evocative Marscapes that may be found in the planet's towering mountains and fog-shrouded canyons. Nor do surface photographs like these show us much of Mars; the landers combined photographed less than one-billionth of the Martian surface— about as much as would be seen of Earth by standing on one spot in the Australian outback and one tiny island in the Aleutians.

In 1981, the *Viking 1* lander was renamed Mutch Memorial Station, in honor of Thomas "Tim" Mutch, a member of the Viking science team and a veteran mountain climber, who was killed in the Himalayas in 1980. NASA inscribed a silver plaque, "Dedicated to the memory of Tim Mutch," and announced its intention to place it on the *Viking* lander if astronauts one day venture to Mars. *NASA Jet Propulsion Laboratory.*

THESE VIEWS OF THE NORTH POLAR CAP of Mars were transmitted to Earth by the *Viking 2* orbiter. The automated spacecraft fired its maneuvering engines on September 30, 1976, altering the plane of its orbit to bring it to 75° latitude, in clear view of the pole. It was summer in the north, and the carbon dioxide ("dry") ice that blankets the pole in winter was gone, exposing a permanent, water-ice polar cap.

The burnished patterns of the Martian landscape portrayed in Photographs 51 and 52 consist of a thin crust of water ice overlying a sandy surface. The small circular feature in Photograph 52 is an impact crater, about eight miles in diameter, sheathed in ice. These regions lie near the edge of the permanent north polar cap.

In Photographs 53 and 54, the exposed surface can be seen interrupting the ice; these fingers form part of a spectacular spiral pattern that embraces the entire polar cap. The pattern is thought to have been created when the climate of Mars was altered by changes in its orbit or in the inclination of the planet's axis of rotation. Mars today is a relatively dry planet, but the erosion of its surface indicates that rivers flowed there in balmier times. Study of the north polar cap may help in understanding the causes of global climatic changes on the earth as well.

Photograph 56 shows the northern extremity of one of the spiral bands of exposed topsoil that cut through the north polar ice. The area covered by the photo is thirty-seven miles wide, and the large cliff at top center

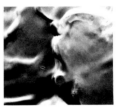

51, 52. POLAR REGION, MARS

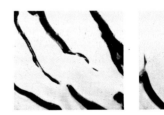

53, 54. ICE CAP, MARS

133

56. POLAR REGION, MARS

57. MARINER VALLEY, MARS
58. DUNES AND SNOWFIELDS

is over sixteen hundred feet high. The terracing along the edge of the polar cap, evidence of long-term climatic changes on Mars, lends the surface its wood-grained look. The terraces, some etched with frost, average about one hundred sixty-five feet thick. The colors were created by combining three black-and-white images taken through red, green, and blue filters; they are as accurate as the Viking technicians knew how to make them. North is at the top, and the sun is shining from the south.

Photograph 57 shows a small segment of the western reaches of Valles Marineris (Mariner Valley). This titanic canyon, the largest in the solar system, is twenty-eight hundred miles long, ninety to four hundred miles wide, and as much as twenty thousand feet deep. Placed in North America it would stretch from Long Island to San Francisco Bay. So large that it can be seen through telescopes on Earth, Mariner Valley enjoys the distinction of being the only true "canal" of Mars; all the other canals, sketched at the telescope by Percival Lowell and other astronomers and cited as possible evidence of a technologically advanced civilization on Mars, have proved to be optical illusions.

Photograph 58 shows an intersection between polar deserts and a field of dark sand dunes at latitude 81° north. The desert is blanketed with dry ice in winter; in this summer scene, some frost persists, toward the north (lower left) portion of the photograph. The sands of Mars, unlike those of most of Earth, are dark in color. NASA *Jet Propulsion Laboratory*.

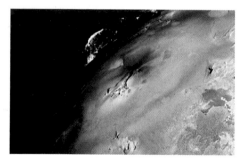

59. IO

JUPITER'S SATELLITE IO, one of the strangest of all known worlds, bristles with furiously active volcanoes. Though Io is only eleven hundred miles in diameter, its volcanos produce the equivalent of the May 1980 eruption of Mount Saint Helens on Earth every month. Some of the volcanic debris—about one ton per second—is ejected so violently that it leaves Io behind as it sails into space. There it arrays itself into a belt that lies along the satellite's orbit. Known as the Io torus, this band of plasma is so pronounced that it can be observed from Earth, four hundred million miles away. Nowhere else in the solar system does such a small object make such a fuss over itelf.

Io's surface would have delighted Dante. Sulphur is the motif. The thin crust appears to be made of solid sulphur. Rock barges, stained sulphur-yellow, float in lava lakes. Volcanos pour yellow sulphur down their black-tar flanks, and geysers of hot liquid sulphur squirt a hundred miles into the sky. At night the scene is further enlivened by the shifting, multicolored glow of never-ending aurorae produced by the torus, and by the sight of Jupiter itself, spread out across fully thirty degrees of the sky.

When the solar system was young, Jupiter would have been so hot that it would resemble a miniature star, bathing Io in more heat than the earth today receives from the sun. In the billions of years since those turbulent times, most of the objects in the solar system have cooled off; the earth's moon, for example, is about the same size as Io, but its epoch of major geological activity ended long ago. Yet Io has found no peace. The reason seems to be that Io is both enthralled by Jupiter's intense gravitational field and locked into a gravitational resonance with its neighboring satellite Europa. Europa perturbs Io's orbit, so that Io is alternately squeezed and relaxed by Jupiter's gravitational field, like a gently pinched grape. The resulting friction has kept Io boiling for eons.

These three Voyager photographs of Io were computer-processed by Alfred McEwen of the U.S. Geological Survey to combine color with high resolution. In Photograph 59 the central feature is Pele, the largest geyser-like volcano found on Io. Caught in the act of erupting, Pele is ejecting a plume nearly two hundred miles high. Part of the plume can be seen at upper right, silhouetted against the black sky. Material splashing back onto the surface of Io forms the dark ring surrounding Pele.

Photograph 60 covers nearly 10 percent of the surface of Io. The scars in the crust are apparently calderas—volcanic craters—and the white spots sulphur dioxide gas and frost. The mountain to the lower left, some thirty thousand feet high, is made of rock of the sort believed to compose Io's silicate crust, most of which is submerged beneath the sulphur oceans. The spidery black formation to the left in Photograph 61 is Ra Patera, a caldera oozing with a jet-black sulphur tar. Bright blue hot spots signal fresh eruptions. *Alfred McEwen, U.S. Geological Survey; NASA Jet Propulsion Laboratory.*

60. IO

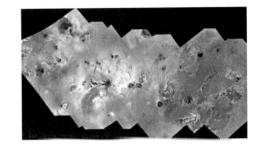

61. IO

THE EARLY-MORNING SUN lights up an unnamed ridge east of Hellas basin in this *Viking* orbiter photograph taken over the southern hemisphere of Mars. About twenty miles of ridgeline can be seen. Hellas itself, out of the frame well to the west, is an old impact crater, nearly a thousand miles wide, molten rock from which may have drowned the craters that once dotted the region in the photograph. Here in the foothills and mountains, the lava appears to have subsided, and the outlines of a few half-swamped craters can be seen in the photograph. *NASA Jet Propulsion Laboratory.*

55. MOUNTAINS OF MARS

135

62. KITT PEAK, ARIZONA

A THUNDERSTORM ROLLING OVER Kitt Peak National Observatory in Arizona was photographed at uncomfortably close range by Gary Ladd in 1972. The mountain, sixty-nine hundred feet high, acted as a natural lightning rod; Ladd took a series of photographs outside, then retreated indoors when a lightning bolt struck close by. He shot this frame through a window in one of the telescope domes, with an exposure of about one minute through a 28mm lens on 35mm color-transparancy film. Reponse to Ladd's photograph was so enthusiastic that he gave up his job as a research assistant at Kitt Peak and became a professional photographer.

The dome at the top of the mountain houses the one-hundred-fifty-eight-inch Mayall telescope, among the world's largest and most effective astronomical instruments. (Photographs 65, 66, and 72 were taken through the Mayall telescope.) Below it and to the right is the dome of a fifty-inch telescope. *Gary Ladd.*

63. ORION NEBULA

SIXTEEN HUNDRED LIGHT YEARS from Earth, the Orion Nebula is the closest at hand of the many glowing clouds of gas that line the spiral arms of our galaxy, the Milky Way. Here, along the spiral arms, new stars are condensing out of interstellar clouds. The young stars in turn light up the surrounding cloud, exciting atoms in the cloud into radiating light, by the same process that activates a neon light. The red hues in the cloud represent emission of energy by atoms of hydrogen, the most abundant atom in the cloud.

Stars are continuing to form in the Orion Nebula; some of them, still swaddled in the heart of the nebula and detectable only by the heat they emit, are estimated to have started shining as little as ten thousand years ago. *David Malin, Anglo-Australian Observatory.*

64. MONOCEROS NEBULA

MOST OF THE VAST CLOUDS OF DUST and gas adrift among the stars of the Milky Way are dark; only at intervals, where they have collapsed to form new stars, are the clouds illuminated. Here, in the constellation Monoceros, a cone-shaped portion of a dark interstellar cloud is silhouetted against a slightly more distant part of the cloud, which blazes with the light of fresh stars. The cone measures approximately six light years in length. (One light year equals the distance light, traveling 186,000 miles per second in a vacuum, travels in one year—some 5,800,000,000,000 miles.) The dark cloud extends well along the Milky Way, and may be part of a complex that involves the Orion Nebula (Photograph 63). This photograph was taken through the two-hundred-inch Hale telescope at Palomar Observatory in southern California. *Palomar Observatory.*

TWO SPIRAL GALAXIES, each composed of over one hundred billion stars, were photographed with the one-hundred-fifty-eight-inch Mayall telescope at Kitt Peak National Observatory. We see Galaxy M104, the "Sombrero" Galaxy (Photograph 65), nearly edge-on; it displays a dark plane of interstellar dust and gas, the same sort of material that makes up the dark clouds of our Milky Way galaxy (see Photograph 64). Most of the bright points of light are foreground stars in our galaxy, but some, more diffuse and clustered around the Sombrero Galaxy, are faint images of a few of its hundreds of globular star clusters. The Sombrero is about forty million light years distant, and probably belongs, as does the Milky Way, to the Virgo supercluster of galaxies.

Galaxy M51 (Photograph 66) lies about thirty to forty million light years from Earth, and presents itself face-on. A second galaxy, NGC 5195, is visible immediately to the left of M51. The two galaxies recently drifted close to each other, and their gravitational interaction has distorted the shape of both. *AURA, Inc., Kitt Peak National Observatory.*

65. GALAXY M104   66. GALAXY M51

THESE TWO SPIRAL GALAXIES, M81 (Photograph 67) and M83 (Photograph 68), lie about ten million light years from our galaxy, itself a spiral. Their spiral arms are not objects, like vines, but phenomena, like the phosphorescence created when ocean waves stir up plankton. The spiral arms glow with the massed light of billions of young giant and supergiant stars and of the surrounding nebulae, from parts of which the stars condensed. The clouds are shocked into collapse by density waves, which in turn are created by gravitational resonances among the billions of stars that compose the galaxy. The density waves propagate outward in a spiral pattern, collapsing the clouds and creating the stars, the light from which traces out the shape of the density wave.

These are negative prints, employed by astronomers who study galaxies because such prints reveal maximum detail. Photograph 67 was made by Milton Humason through the one-hundred-inch Hooker telescope at Mount Wilson Observatory in California, the instrument with which Humason and Edwin Hubble made pioneering studies of the expansion of the universe. Photograph 68 was taken with the one-hundred-inch DuPont telescope at Las Campanas Observatory in Chile, by Allan Sandage, once Hubble's student. *Carnegie Institution of Washington, Mount Wilson and Las Campanas Observatories.*

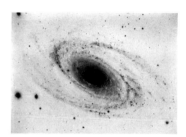

67. GALAXY M81

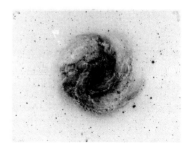

68. GALAXY M83

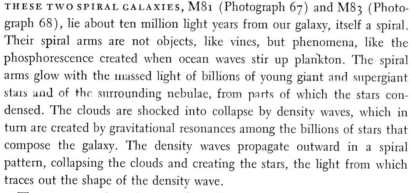

137

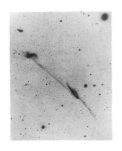
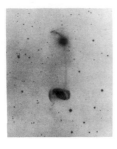

69, 70. INTERACTING GALAXIES

HALTON ARP of the Mount Wilson and Las Campanas Observatories has long studied peculiar-looking galaxies, many of which have been distorted by gravitational interaction with neighboring galaxies. In the course of such interactions, millions of stars can be stripped from one galaxy and acquired by another or flung off into intergalactic space. The galaxies are black against a white sky in these negative prints, made from plates taken by Arp with the two-hundred-inch Hale telescope at Palomar Observatory. Photograph 69 is of IC 1505 (number 295 in Arp's *Atlas of Peculiar Galaxies*); Photograph 70 shows NGC 5216/18 (Arp 104). *Halton Arp, Carnegie Institution of Washington, Mount Wilson and Las Campanas Observatories.*

71. VEIL NEBULA

THE VEIL NEBULA (NGC 6960), fifteen hundred light years away in the constellation Cygnus, is part of a shell of gas cast off in the explosion of a star some thirty to forty thousand years ago. As it expands, the bubble is becoming entangled with interstellar clouds. Eventually it will have mingled completely with these clouds—the stuff of a dead star, recycled into the galaxy to become part of future stars. *Carnegie Institution of Washington, Mount Wilson and Las Campanas Observatories.*

72. TRIFID NEBULA

BRIGHT NEBULAE like the Trifid (Photograph 72) and the Orion Nebula (Photograph 63) have a three-dimensional structure that can be seen especially clearly in the case of the Trifid; stars shining inside this ball of gas illuminate it from within. The blue and red hues result from the various degrees to which hydrogen atoms in the gas cloud have absorbed, then emitted, energy radiated by the stars in the nebula. The Trifid is part of a large interstellar cloud lining the Sagittarius arm of our galaxy, which lies about fifteen hundred light years away in the direction of the center of our galaxy. This photograph was taken with the one-hundred-fifty-eight-inch Mayall telescope at Kitt Peak National Observatory. *AURA, Inc., Kitt Peak National Observatory.*

LIKE THE ANDROMEDA GALAXY (Photograph 74), our Milky Way is orbited by two satellite galaxies, each home to billions of stars. The large Magellanic Cloud, the more formidable of these companions, lies near the plane of our galaxy and toward its far side; therefore we see it through a dence thicket of Milky Way stars. The stars of the Large Magellanic Cloud compose the vaguely oval structure that runs diagonally across the center of the frame. The ruddy blossom to the left is the largest known bright nebula, similar to the Orion Nebula (Photograph 63) but much larger. The distance of the cloud is some one hundred and fifty thousand light years.

The subtle colors of the cloud are captured with unprecedented accuracy in this print, made by Claus Madsen from plates taken with the wide-angle Schmidt telescope of the European Southern Observatory in Geneva. *European Southern Observatory*.

73. MAGELLANIC CLOUD

THE ANDROMEDA GALAXY, sister galaxy to our Milky Way, is only two and a quarter million light years distant—so close that it can be seen by the unaided eye on clear, moonless nights in the northern hemisphere. Two satellite galaxies orbit Andromeda. One appears to the lower right of the photograph. The other, at the upper left, peers through the far outer edge of the galactic disk. The disk itself is warped, tilting up somewhat at the left and down at the right, an effect probably produced by the gravitational tug of the Milky Way.

The yellow glow at the center of the galaxy is produced by billions of middle-aged stars like the sun, while the blue hues of the outer disk bespeak the presence of young blue-white stars formed in recent epochs along the spiral arms. This color photograph was produced by William Miller from plates taken at Palomar Observatory; a discussion of Miller's work appears in the Introduction. *California Institute of Technology*.

74. GALAXY M31

THE ROTATION OF THE EARTH turned the stars' images into trails during this four-hour time exposure, made in southern-hemisphere summer, 1980, from Cerro Tololo Inter-American Observatory in the Chilean Andes. The view is toward the south celestial pole. The skies in Chile are among the clearest in the world, and the colors of the brighter stars inscribed themselves vividly on the 35mm transparency film. The bright streak to the left is a meteor, and the red strip to the right was produced by red night-vision lights inside the telescope dome. *Douglas Kirkland*.

75. STAR TRAILS

76. ASTRONAUT AND COSMONAUT

ASTRONAUT DONALD "DEKE" SLAYTON and cosmonaut Aleksey Leonov posed in weightlessness in the *Soyuz* orbital module during the joint Apollo-Soyuz mission of July, 1975. Slayton had been one of the original Gemini astronauts sixteen years earlier, but this was his first spaceflight. A heart problem had kept him earthbound for more than a decade before he finally convinced cardiologists to recertify him for space. Leonov, something of a Russian folk hero, was the first man to walk in space, on a Voskhod mission during which he twice narrowly escaped death. Finding himself unable to reenter his spacecraft at the conclusion of the spacewalk, Leonov took the drastic step of reducing the pressure in his suit to only four pounds per square inch, a measure that risked his suffering the agonies of the bends, brought on by nitrogen bubbles in the bloodstream. This action enabled him to squeeze back through the hatch to safety. Then, when he and cosmonaut Pavel Belyayev reentered the atmosphere, they missed their landing site by two thousand miles and spent a frigid night in a birch forest in the Urals. Wolves circled their spacecraft while rescue crews searched for it. Four years later, Leonov was riding in a parade in Moscow when his car was sprayed with bullets by a would-be assassin, who evidently mistook one of his fellow cosmonauts for Leonid Brezhnev. Again Leonov escaped injury.

Compared to these exploits, the Apollo-Soyuz mission was tame. Cosmonauts Leonov and Valery Kubasov and astronauts Slayton, Thomas Stafford, and Vance Brand trained together for two years, learning the rudiments of each other's languages and posing for publicity photographs perched on spacecraft models in Houston or busy planting trees in Tashkent.

Then, on July 15, *Soyuz-19* was launched into a parking orbit at an altitude of one hundred twenty miles. As the rotation of the earth brought Cape Canaveral beneath the *Soyuz* orbit, *Apollo* was launched. It caught up with *Soyuz* in a little over a day. The ships docked, and the astronauts and cosmonauts made their way through a connecting airlock to shake hands; the moment was broadcast over live television in both countries. Asked about the relative merits of American and Soviet space food, Leonov replied smoothly, "It is not what you eat but with whom you eat that is important."

Born in a lighthearted exchange during a 1961 summit meeting when President John F. Kennedy said, "Let's go to the moon together," and Soviet Premier Nikita Khrushchev replied, "Why not?" Apollo-Soyuz was meant to symbolize the spirit of détente. "If we continue to live with this friendliness, it will benefit all of us," said cosmonaut Kubasov. "Just like you, I want my children to sleep peacefully and calmly." But détente faded, and Apollo-Soyuz remains the sole joint U.S.–U.S.S.R. mission in the history of spaceflight. *NASA Johnson Space Center.*

THE APOLLO 11 MISSION, the first to land men on the moon (Photographs 19, 31) paused in Earth orbit for one and a half revolutions, then refired its third-stage engine and departed for the moon at a velocity of nearly 25,000 miles per hour. The three astronauts aboard watched bemusedly as the earth dwindled in size, sometimes observing their home planet through a monocular that they could keep steady by letting it float untouched in the weightlessness of their cabin.

"I am conscious of distance," astronaut Michael Collins recalled. "Distance *away from home*. It is a sobering, almost melancholy, sight, this shrinking globe, and for the first time in my life I think I know what 'outward bound' means."

This photograph was taken when *Apollo 11* was 112,000 statute miles out. The Mediterranean Sea, the Red Sea, the Persian Gulf, and most of the Arabian Sea are visible, as is much of Arabia and Africa, basking in the heat of a July afternoon. Night has already fallen in India, lost in darkness to the right. NASA *Johnson Space Center*.

77. EARTH

AS THEY WANDER IN from the outer reaches of the solar system, new comets are often discovered not by professional astronomers but by amateurs. That was the case with Comet Bennett, first spotted by John Bennett of Pretoria, South Africa, on December 28, 1969, while he was sweeping the skies with an old Moonwatch "elbow" telescope, designed for logging early artificial satellites. One of the brightest and most gracefullooking comets of recent decades, Comet Bennett grew a luxuriant tail as it approached the sun. (For more on comets, see Photograph 49.) This photograph was taken by Akira Fujii on April 3, 1970, using a guided 35mm camera with a 100mm lens on transparency film at ƒ/2.8. *Akira Fujii*.

78. COMET BENNETT

Further Reading

ABLE GENERAL INTRODUCTIONS to astronomy include *The Cambridge Encyclopaedia of Astronomy*, edited by Simon Mitton; *Exploration of the Universe*, by George Abell; *Astronomy: The Cosmic Journey*, by William Hartmann; and *Contemporary Astronomy*, by Jay Pasachoff. On the solar system, see *The New Solar System*, edited by J. Kelly Beatty, Brian O'Leary, and Andrew Chaikin; *Orbiting the Sun*, by Fred Whipple; and *Daytime Star*, by Simon Mitton. Among the reliable semitechnical surveys of planetary geology are *Introduction to Planetary Geology*, by Billy Glass; and *Earthlike Planets*, by Bruce Murray, Michael Malin, and Ronald Greeley.

Cosmological questions are surveyed in *Cosmology: The Science of the Universe*, by Edward Harrison; while the evolution of the very early universe is reviewed in nontechnical terms in *The Left Hand of Creation*, by John Barrow and Joseph Silk, *The Moment of Creation*, by James Trefil, and *The First Three Minutes*, by Steven Weinberg. For studies of life and intelligence in the context of cosmic evolution, see *Life Beyond Earth*, by Gerald Feinberg and Robert Shapiro, and *Intelligent Life in the Universe*, by I. S. Shklovskii and Carl Sagan.

Some of the topics discussed in the introduction to this book are explored in *Kandinsky: Complete Writings on Art*, edited by Kenneth Lindsay and Peter Vergo; *The New Landscape*, by Gyorgy Kepes; *Structure in Art and in Science*, by Gyorgy Kepes; *A Search for Structure*, by Cyril Stanley Smith; *Paul Klee: Notebooks*, edited by Jurg Spiller; *Modern Art and Scientific*

Thought, by John Adkins Richardson; and *Patterns in Nature,* by Peter Stevens.

Astronomical photographs are collected in *The Cambridge Photographic Atlas of the Planets,* by G. A. Briggs and F. W. Taylor; *The New Astronomy,* by Nigel Henbest and Michael Marten; *The Hubble Atlas of Galaxies,* by Allan Sandage; *Pictorial Astronomy,* by Dinsmore Alter and Clarence Cleminshaw; and *Galaxies,* by Timothy Ferris.

About the Author

TIMOTHY FERRIS'S BOOKS include *The Red Limit: The Search for the Edge of the Universe*; *Galaxies*; *Murmurs of Earth*, with Carl Sagan *et al.*; and a textbook, *Journalism: An Introduction to Newswriting and Reporting*, with Bruce Porter. At present, he is writing a study of the history and philosophy of science titled *Coming of Age in the Milky Way*. Articles by Ferris have appeared in over a hundred newspapers and in magazines including the *New York Times Magazine*, *Esquire*, *Geo*, *Harper's*, *Science*, *Science Digest*, *Readers' Digest*, *Discover*, and *Rolling Stone*, where for eight years he was a contributing editor.

Ferris produced the Voyager phonograph record, launched aboard twin interstellar spacecraft in 1977. His commentaries on science are heard over National Public Radio, and he is a regular contributor to the *New York Times Book Review*. He is currently visiting professor at the University of Southern California School of Journalism.

圖二三 天 文 圖（摹本）